THE LARGE CATECHISM

of

MARTIN LUTHER

Translated by

ROBERT H. FISCHER

FORTRESS PRESS   PHILADELPHIA

Library of Congress Catalog Card Number 61-3802

ISBN 0-8006-0885-2

Eighth printing 1985

1795A85   Printed in the United States of America   1-885

FOREWORD

This separate publication of Luther's Large Catechism is taken from *The Book of Concord,* translated and edited by Theodore G. Tappert in collaboration with Jaroslav Pelikan, Robert H. Fischer, and Arthur C. Piepkorn (Philadelphia: Fortress Press, 1959). The translation of the Large Catechism is by Robert H. Fischer.

All cross-references in the footnotes are to articles (or chapters) and sections. Sections are indicated in the right margins of the text. A few commonly accepted abbreviations have been employed in the footnotes: *WA* for the Weimar edition of Luther's works, *EA* for the Erlangen edition of Luther's works, *C.R.* for the *Corpus Reformatorum* containing works of Reformers other than Luther.

For most quotations from the Bible, the Revised Standard Version has been used as on the whole closest to the rendering in the text, but where the context requires it other versions or literal translations have been used.

CONTENTS

INTRODUCTION 1

MARTIN LUTHER'S PREFACE. 2

PREFACE 6

FIRST PART: THE TEN COMMANDMENTS 9

SECOND PART: THE CREED 55

THIRD PART: THE LORD'S PRAYER 64

FOURTH PART: BAPTISM 80

FIFTH PART: THE SACRAMENT OF THE ALTAR 91

A BRIEF EXHORTATION TO CONFESSION 101

THE LARGE CATECHISM
of
Dr. Martin Luther

INTRODUCTION

Once the Evangelical churches had achieved some external stability, the need was to strengthen them internally. Luther had already produced a number of sermons and pamphlets, beginning as far back as 1516, to present popular instruction on basic elements of Christian doctrine. In 1525 he assigned to his friends Justus Jonas and John Agricola the task of composing a book of religious instruction for children, which he referred to as a "catechism." When this work suffered delay, as did also an attempt in 1528 by Philip Melanchthon, Luther took the initiative again. He assigned to Melanchthon the composition of the "Instruction to the Visitors of the Clergy in the Electorate of Saxony" (1528) while he himself undertook the preparation of a catechism.

The immediate background material consists of three series of sermons which Luther preached in May, September, and November-December, 1528, and March, 1529. Before these sermons were ended Luther was at work writing the Large Catechism. Parts of it were sent to the press before the whole was completed, which helps to explain the discrepancies in the text of the Ten Commandments.

In April, 1529, the "German Catechism" appeared, printed by George Rhaw in Wittenberg. (The title "Large Catechism" is not Luther's.) Later the same year Luther issued a revised edition which added an "Exhortation to Confession," a lengthy insertion in the introduction to the explanation of the Lord's Prayer, and several marginal notes. This edition was the first to be illustrated, some of the cuts coming from Lucas Cranach the Elder. Another edition appeared in 1530, furnished with a second and longer preface which had probably been composed at the Coburg. The last revision corrected by Luther himself came out in 1538.

A Latin translation of the Large Catechism appeared in 1529 and a second edition in 1544, the work of a humanist, Vincent Obsopoeus,

1

who undertook to make of it a stylistic showpiece by adorning it with classical citations and allusions to ancient history. Otherwise it is generally a slavish translation of Luther's German. It was not necessary, therefore, to reproduce here the Latin variations from the German text.

MARTIN LUTHER'S PREFACE[1]

It is not for trivial reasons that we constantly treat the Catechism and strongly urge others to do the same. For we see to our sorrow that many pastors and preachers[2] are very negligent in this respect and despise both their office and this teaching itself. Some because of their great and lofty learning, others because of sheer laziness and gluttony, behave in this matter as if they were pastors or preachers for their bellies' sake and had nothing to do but live off the fat of the land all their days, as they used to do under the papacy.

Everything that they are to teach and preach is now available 2 to them in clear and simple form in the many excellent books which are in reality what the old manuals claimed in their titles to be: "Sermons That Preach Themselves," "Sleep Soundly," "Prepared!" and "Treasury." [3] However, they are not so upright and honest as to buy these books, or if they have them, to examine and read them. Such shameful gluttons and servants of their bellies would make better swineherds or dogkeepers than spiritual guides and pastors.

Now that they are free from the useless, bothersome babbling of 3 the Seven Hours,[4] it would be fine if every morning, noon, and evening they would read, instead, at least a page or two from the Catechism, the Prayer Book,[5] the New Testament, or something else from the Bible and would pray the Lord's Prayer for themselves and their parishioners. In this way they might show honor and gratitude to the Gospel, through which they have been delivered from so many burdens and troubles, and they might feel a little shame because, like pigs and dogs, they remember no more of the Gospel than this rotten,

---

[1] In the German edition of the Book of Concord, 1580, this Longer Preface (which dates from 1530) appeared after the Shorter Preface in accordance with the order observed in the fourth German volume of the Jena edition of Luther's Works (1556).

[2] Preachers (*Prediger*) were limited to preaching; pastors (*Pfarrherren*) exercised the full ministerial office.

[3] Titles of medieval sermon books.

[4] The seven canonical hours, daily prayers prescribed by the medieval Breviary.

[5] Luther published the "Little Prayer Book" (*Betbüchlein*) in 1522 to replace Roman Catholic devotional books.

pernicious, shameful, carnal liberty. As it is, the common people 4
take the Gospel altogether too lightly, and even our utmost exertions
accomplish but little. What, then, can we expect if we are sluggish
and lazy, as we used to be under the papacy?

Besides, a shameful and insidious plague of security and bore- 5
dom has overtaken us. Many regard the Catechism as a simple, silly
teaching which they can absorb and master at one reading. After
reading it once they toss the book into a corner as if they are ashamed
to read it again. Indeed, even among the nobility there are some 6
louts and skinflints who declare that we can do without pastors and
preachers from now on because we have everything in books and can
learn it all by ourselves. So they blithely let parishes fall into decay,
and brazenly allow both pastors and preachers to suffer distress and
hunger. This is what one can expect of crazy Germans. We Germans
have such disgraceful people among us and must put up with them.

As for myself, let me say that I, too, am a doctor and a preacher 7
—yes, and as learned and experienced as any of those who act so
high and mighty. Yet I do as a child who is being taught the Catechism. Every morning, and whenever else I have time, I read and
recite word for word the Lord's Prayer, the Ten Commandments, the
Creed, the Psalms, etc. I must still read and study the Catechism 8
daily, yet I cannot master it as I wish, but must remain a child and
pupil of the Catechism, and I do it gladly. These dainty, fastidious
fellows would like quickly, with one reading, to become doctors above
all doctors, to know all there is to be known. Well, this, too, is a
sure sign that they despise both their office and the people's souls, yes,
even God and his Word. They need not fear a fall, for they have
already fallen all too horribly. What they need is to become children
and begin learning their ABC's, which they think they have outgrown
long ago.

Therefore, I beg these lazy-bellies and presumptuous saints, 9
for God's sake, to get it into their heads that they are not really and
truly such learned and great doctors as they think. I implore them
not to imagine that they have learned these parts of the Catechism
perfectly, or at least sufficiently, even though they think they know
them ever so well. Even if their knowledge of the Catechism were
perfect (though that is impossible in this life), yet it is highly profitable
and fruitful daily to read it and make it the subject of meditation and
conversation. In such reading, conversation, and meditation the Holy
Spirit is present and bestows ever new and greater light and fervor, so
that day by day we relish and appreciate the Catechism more greatly.
This is according to Christ's promise in Matt. 18:20, "Where two or
three are gathered in my name, there am I in the midst of them."

Nothing is so effectual against the devil, the world, the flesh, 10
and all evil thoughts as to occupy oneself with the Word of God, talk

about it, and meditate on it. Psalm 1 calls those blessed who "meditate on God's law day and night." [6] You will never offer up any incense or other savor more potent against the devil than to occupy yourself with God's commandments and words and to speak, sing, and meditate on them. This, indeed, is the true holy water, the sign which routs the devil and puts him to flight.[7]

For this reason alone you should eagerly read, recite, ponder, 11 and practice the Catechism, even if the only blessing and benefit you obtain from it is to rout the devil and evil thoughts. For he cannot bear to hear God's Word. God's Word is not like some empty tale, such as the one about Dietrich of Bern,[8] but as St. Paul says in Rom. 1:16, it is "the power of God," indeed, the power of God which burns the devil and gives us immeasurable strength, comfort, and help.

Why should I waste words? Time and paper would fail me if I 12 were to recount all the blessings that flow from God's Word. The devil is called the master of a thousand arts. What, then, shall we call God's Word, which routs and destroys this master of a thousand arts with all his wiles and might? It must, indeed, be master of more than a hundred thousand arts. Shall we frivolously despise this 13 might, blessing, power, and fruit—especially we who would be pastors and preachers? If so, we deserve not only to be refused food but also to be chased out by dogs and pelted with dung. Not only do we need God's Word daily as we need our daily bread; we also must use it daily against the daily, incessant attacks and ambushes of the devil with his thousand arts.

If this were not enough to admonish us to read the Catechism 14 daily, there is God's command. That alone should be incentive enough. Deut. 6:7, 8 solemnly enjoins that we should always meditate upon his precepts whether sitting, walking, standing, lying down, or rising, and keep them before our eyes and in our hands as a constant token and sign. Certainly God did not require and command this so solemnly without good reason. He knows our danger and need. He knows the constant and furious attacks and assaults of the devil. So he wishes to warn, equip, and protect us against them with good "armor" against their "flaming darts," [9] and with a good antidote against their evil infection and poison. O what mad, senseless 15 fools we are! We must ever live and dwell in the midst of such mighty enemies as the devils, and yet we despise our weapons and armor, too lazy to give them a thought!

[6] Ps. 1:2.

[7] I.e., the Word of God really does what holy water was formerly believed to accomplish.

[8] Luther frequently cited the legend of Dietrich of Bern as an example of lies and fables.

[9] Eph. 6:11, 16.

Look at these bored, presumptuous saints who will not or can- 16
not read and study the Catechism daily. They evidently consider
themselves much wiser than God himself, and wiser than all his holy
angels, prophets, apostles, and all Christians! God himself is not
ashamed to teach it daily, for he knows of nothing better to teach,
and he always keeps on teaching this one thing without varying it
with anything new or different. All the saints know of nothing better
or different to learn, though they cannot learn it to perfection. Are we
not most marvelous fellows, therefore, if we imagine, after reading
or hearing it once, that we know it all and need not read or study it
any more? Most marvelous fellows, to think we can finish learning
in one hour what God himself cannot finish teaching! Actually, he is
busy teaching it from the beginning of the world to the end, and all
prophets and saints have been busy learning it and have always remained pupils, and must continue to do so.

This much is certain: anyone who knows the Ten Command- 17
ments perfectly knows the entire Scriptures. In all affairs and circumstances he can counsel, help, comfort, judge, and make decisions in
both spiritual and temporal matters. He is qualified to sit in judgment
upon all doctrines, estates, persons, laws, and everything else in the
world.

What is the whole Psalter but meditations and exercises based 18
on the First Commandment? Now, I know beyond a doubt that such
lazy-bellies and presumptuous fellows do not understand a single
Psalm, much less the entire Scriptures, yet they pretend to know and
despise the Catechism, which is a brief compend and summary of all
the Holy Scriptures.

Therefore, I once again implore all Christians, especially pastors 19
and preachers, not to try to be doctors prematurely and to imagine
that they know everything. Vain imaginations, like new cloth, suffer
shrinkage! Let all Christians exercise themselves in the Catechism
daily, and constantly put it into practice, guarding themselves with the
greatest care and diligence against the poisonous infection of such
security or vanity. Let them continue to read and teach, to learn and
meditate and ponder. Let them never stop until they have proved by
experience that they have taught the devil to death and have become
wiser than God himself and all his saints.

If they show such diligence, then I promise them—and their 20
experience will bear me out—that they will gain much fruit and God
will make excellent men of them. Then in due time they themselves
will make the noble confession that the longer they work with the
Catechism, the less they know of it and the more they have to learn.
Only then, hungry and thirsty, will they truly relish what now they
cannot bear to smell because they are so bloated and surfeited. To
this end may God grant his grace! Amen.

PREFACE[1]

This sermon has been undertaken for the instruction of children |
and uneducated people. Hence from ancient times it has been called,
in Greek, a "catechism"—that is, instruction for children. Its   2
contents represent the minimum of knowledge required of a Christian.
Whoever does not possess it should not be reckoned among Christians
nor admitted to a sacrament,[2] just as a craftsman who does not know
the rules and practices of his craft is rejected and considered incom-
petent. For this reason young people should be thoroughly in-   3
structed in the various parts of the Catechism or children's sermons
and diligently drilled in their practice.

Therefore, it is the duty of every head of a household to examine   4
his children and servants at least once a week and ascertain what they
have learned of it, and if they do not know it, to keep them faithfully
at it. I well remember the time when there were old people who   5
were so ignorant that they knew nothing of these things—indeed,
even now we find them daily—yet they come to Baptism and the
Sacrament of the Altar and exercise all the rights of Christians, although those who come to the sacrament ought to know more and
have a fuller understanding of all Christian doctrine than children and
beginners at school. As for the common people, however, we   6
should be satisfied if they learned the three parts[3] which have been
the heritage of Christendom from ancient times, though they were
rarely taught and treated correctly, so that all who wish to be Christians in fact as well as in name, both young and old, may be well-
trained in them and familiar with them.

I. THE TEN COMMANDMENTS OF GOD

1. You shall have no other gods before me. |
2. You shall not take the name of God in vain.   2
3. You shall keep the Sabbath day holy.   3
4. You shall honor father and mother.   4
5. You shall not kill.   5
6. You shall not commit adultery.   6
7. You shall not steal.   7
8. You shall not bear false witness against your neighbor.   8

---

[1] The Shorter Preface is based on a sermon of May 18, 1528 (*WA*, 30I:2).

[2] This was not only a proposal of Luther, but also a medieval prescription;
cf. John Surgant, *Manuale Curatorum* (1502), etc.

[3] Ten Commandments, Creed, Lord's Prayer. From 1525 on catechetical
instruction in Wittenberg was expanded to include material on Baptism and
the Lord's Supper.

9. You shall not covet your neighbor's house.   9
10. You shall not covet his wife, man-servant, maid-servant, cattle,
    or anything that is his.[4]   10

II. THE CHIEF ARTICLES OF OUR FAITH

I believe in God, the Father almighty, maker of heaven and   11
earth:

And in Jesus Christ, his only Son, our Lord: who was conceived   12
by the Holy Spirit, born of the virgin Mary, suffered under Pontius
Pilate, was crucified, dead, and buried: he descended into hell, the
third day he rose from the dead, he ascended into heaven, and sits on
the right hand of God, the Father almighty, whence he shall come
to judge the living and the dead.

I believe in the Holy Spirit, the holy Christian church,[5] the   13
communion of saints, the forgiveness of sins, the resurrection of the
body, and the life everlasting. Amen.

III. THE PRAYER, OR OUR FATHER, WHICH CHRIST TAUGHT

Our Father who art in heaven, hallowed be thy name. Thy   14
kingdom come, thy will be done, on earth as it is in heaven. Give us
this day our daily bread; and forgive us our debts, as we also have
forgiven our debtors; and lead us not into temptation, but deliver us
from evil. For thine is the kingdom and the power and the glory,
forever. Amen.[6]

These are the most necessary parts of Christian instruction.   15
We should learn to repeat them word for word. Our children   16
should be taught the habit of reciting them daily when they rise in
the morning, when they go to their meals, and when they go to bed
at night; until they repeat them they should not be given anything
to eat or drink. Every father has the same duty to his household;   17
he should dismiss man-servants and maid-servants if they do not know
these things and are unwilling to learn them. Under no circum-   18
stances should a person be tolerated if he is so rude and unruly that
he refuses to learn these three parts in which everything contained in
Scripture is comprehended in short, plain, and simple terms, for   19
the dear fathers or apostles, whoever they were,[7] have thus summed
up the doctrine, life, wisdom, and learning which constitute the Christian's conversation, conduct, and concern.

[4] Ex. 20:2-17; cf. Deut. 5:6-21.
[5] The translation of *ecclesiam catholicam* by *eine christliche Kirche* was
common in fifteenth century Germany.
[6] Matt. 6:9-13; cf. Luke 11:2-4.
[7] Luther was not interested in defending the apostolic authorship of the
Creed.

When these three parts are understood, we ought also to know   20
what to say about the sacraments which Christ himself instituted,
Baptism and the holy Body and Blood of Christ, according to the
texts of Matthew and Mark at the end of their Gospels where they
describe how Christ said farewell to his disciples and sent them forth.

BAPTISM   21

"Go and teach all nations, and baptize them in the name of the
Father and of the Son and of the Holy Spirit" (Matt. 28:19). "He
who believes and is baptized will be saved; but he who does not believe
will be condemned" (Mark 16:16).

It is enough for an ordinary person to know this much about   22
Baptism from the Scriptures. The other sacrament may be dealt with
similarly, in short, simple words according to the text of St. Paul.

THE SACRAMENT [OF THE ALTAR]   23

"Our Lord Jesus Christ on the night when he was betrayed took
bread, gave thanks, and broke it and gave it to his disciples, saying,
'Take and eat, this is my body, which is given for you. Do this in
remembrance of me.'

"In the same way also the cup, after supper, saying, 'This cup is
the new testament in my blood, which is shed for you for the forgiveness of sins. Do this, as often as you drink it, in remembrance of me'"
(I Cor. 11:23-25).

Thus we have, in all, five parts covering the whole of Christian   24
doctrine, which we should constantly teach and require young people
to recite word for word. Do not assume that they will learn and retain
this teaching from sermons alone. When these parts have been   25
well learned, you may assign them also some Psalms or some hymns,[8]
based on these subjects, to supplement and confirm their knowledge.
Thus our youth will be led into the Scriptures so that they make
progress daily.

However, it is not enough for them simply to learn and repeat   26
these parts verbatim. The young people should also attend preaching,
especially at the time designated for the Catechism,[9] so that they may
hear it explained and may learn the meaning of every part. Then they
will also be able to repeat what they have heard and give a good,
correct answer when they are questioned, and thus the preaching will
not be without benefit and fruit. The reason we take such care to   27
preach on the Catechism frequently is to impress it upon our youth,
not in a lofty and learned manner but briefly and very simply, so that
it may penetrate deeply into their minds and remain fixed in their
memories.

[8] Luther himself wrote six hymns based on the parts of the Catechism.
[9] Preaching and instruction on the Catechism especially during Lent.

Now we shall take up the above-mentioned parts one by one 28
and in the plainest possible manner say about them as much as is
necessary.

[FIRST PART: THE TEN COMMANDMENTS]

THE FIRST COMMANDMENT

"You shall have no other gods."

That is, you shall regard me alone as your God. What does this |
mean, and how is it to be understood? What is it to have a god? What
is God?

Answer: A god is that to which we look for all good and in 2
which we find refuge in every time of need. To have a god is nothing
else than to trust and believe him with our whole heart. As I have
often said, the trust and faith of the heart alone make both God and
an idol. If your faith and trust are right, then your God is the 3
true God. On the other hand, if your trust is false and wrong, then
you have not the true God. For these two belong together, faith and
God. That to which your heart clings and entrusts itself is, I say,
really your God.

The purpose of this commandment, therefore, is to require true 4
faith and confidence of the heart, and these fly straight to the one
true God and cling to him alone. The meaning is: "See to it that
you let me alone be your God, and never seek another." In other
words: "Whatever good thing you lack, look to me for it and seek it
from me, and whenever you suffer misfortune and distress, come and
cling to me. I am the one who will satisfy you and help you out of
every need. Only let your heart cling to no one else."

This I must explain a little more plainly, so that it may be 5
understood and remembered, by citing some common examples of
failure to observe this commandment. Many a person thinks he has
God and everything he needs when he has money and property; in
them he trusts and of them he boasts so stubbornly and securely that he
cares for no one. Surely such a man also has a god—mammon[1] by 6
name, that is, money and possessions—on which he fixes his whole
heart. It is the most common idol on earth. He who has money and 7
property feels secure, happy, fearless, as if he were sitting in the midst
of paradise. On the other hand, he who has nothing doubts and 8
despairs as if he never heard of God. Very few there are who are 9
cheerful, who do not fret and complain, if they do not have mammon.

---

[1] Cf. Matt. 6:24.

This desire for wealth clings and cleaves to our nature all the way to the grave.

So, too, if anyone boasts of great learning, wisdom, power, 10 prestige, family, and honor, and trusts in them, he also has a god, but not the one, true God. Notice, again, how presumptuous, secure, and proud people become because of such possessions, and how despondent when they lack them or are deprived of them. Therefore, I repeat, to have a God properly means to have something in which the heart trusts completely.

Again, consider what we used to do in our blindness under the 11 papacy. If anyone had a toothache, he fasted to the honor ot St. Apollonia; if he feared fire, he sought St. Lawrence as his patron; if he feared the plague, he made a vow to St. Sebastian or Roch.[2] There were countless other such abominations, and every person selected his own saint and worshiped and invoked him in time of need. In this 12 class belong those who go so far as to make a pact with the devil in order that he may give them plenty of money, help them in love affairs, protect their cattle, recover lost possessions, etc., as magicians and sorcerers do. All these fix their heart and trust elsewhere than in the true God. They neither expect nor seek anything from him.

Thus you can easily understand the nature and scope of this 13 commandment. It requires that man's whole heart and confidence be placed in God alone, and in no one else. To have God, you see, does not mean to lay hands upon him, or put him into a purse, or shut him up in a chest. We lay hold of him when our heart embraces him 14 and clings to him. To cling to him with all our heart is nothing 15 else than to entrust ourselves to him completely. He wishes to turn us away from everything else, and to draw us to himself, because he is the one, eternal good. It is as if he said: "What you formerly sought from the saints, or what you hoped to receive from mammon or anything else, turn to me for all this; look upon me as the one who wishes to help you and to lavish all good upon you richly."

Behold, here you have the true honor and the true worship which 16 please God and which he commands under penalty of eternal wrath, namely, that the heart should know no other consolation or confidence than that in him, nor let itself be torn from him, but for him should risk and disregard everything else on earth. On the other hand, 17 you can easily judge how the world practices nothing but false worship

---

[2] On Feb. 9, 248 or 249, Apollonia was martyred, her teeth being knocked out; the medieval church therefore considered her a help against toothache. Lawrence was martyred by burning on Aug. 10, 258. Sebastian was put to death by arrows on Jan. 20, early in the fourth century (?). Roch, who died in 1327, gave himself to care for plague victims. Cf. Luther's first extended exposition of the Ten Commandments (1518) for references to these and other saints, and to magicians and sorcerers. Contemporaries of Luther such as Erasmus also ridiculed this cult of saints.

and idolatry. There has never been a people so wicked that it did not establish and maintain some sort of worship. Everyone has set up a god of his own, to which he looked for blessings, help, and comfort.

For example, the heathen who put their trust in power and 18 dominion exalted Jupiter as their supreme god. Others who strove for riches, happiness, pleasure, and a life of ease venerated Hercules, Mercury, Venus, or others, while pregnant women worshiped Diana or Lucina,[3] and so forth. Everyone made into a god that to which his heart was inclined. Even in the mind of all the heathen, therefore, to have a god means to trust and believe. The trouble is that their 19 trust is false and wrong, for it is not founded upon the one God, apart from whom there is truly no god in heaven or on earth. Accordingly the heathen actually fashion their fancies and dreams 20 about God into an idol and entrust themselves to an empty nothing. So it is with all idolatry. Idolatry does not consist merely of 21 erecting an image and praying to it. It is primarily in the heart, which pursues other things and seeks help and consolation from creatures, saints, or devils. It neither cares for God nor expects good things from him sufficiently to trust that he wants to help, nor does it believe that whatever good it receives comes from God.

There is, moreover, another false worship. This is the greatest 22 idolatry that has been practiced up to now, and it is still prevalent in the world. Upon it all the religious orders are founded. It concerns only that conscience which seeks help, comfort, and salvation in its own works and presumes to wrest heaven from God. It keeps account how often it has made endowments, fasted, celebrated Mass, etc. On such things it relies and of them it boasts, unwilling to receive anything as a gift from God, but desiring by itself to earn or merit everything by works of supererogation, just as if God were in our service or debt and we were his liege lords. What is this but making God into an 23 idol—indeed, an "apple-god" [4]—and setting up ourselves as God? This reasoning, however, is a little too subtle to be understood by young pupils.

This much, however, should be said to ordinary people so that 24 they may mark well and remember the meaning of this commandment: We are to trust in God alone and turn to him, expecting from him only good things; for it is he who gives us body, life, food, drink, nourishment, health, protection, peace, and all temporal and eternal blessings. It is he who protects us from evil, he who saves and

[3] Lucina was the Roman goddess of birth, often identified with Juno.
[4] "Apfelgott" is possibly a corruption of "Aftergott," sham god. Luther speaks of "Apfelkönige oder gemalete Herrn" (WA, 31I:234), the latter expression, literally "painted lords," being a term of derision somewhat like "plaster saint." Sebastian Franck uses the term "Apfelkaiser." The "Apfelbischof" was a Shrove Tuesday character in parts of Germany.

delivers us when any evil befalls. It is God alone, I have often enough repeated, from whom we receive all that is good and by whom we are delivered from all evil. This, I think, is why we Germans 25 from ancient times have called God by a name more elegant and worthy than any found in other languages, a name derived from the word "good" [5] because he is an eternal fountain which overflows with sheer goodness and pours forth all that is good in name and in fact.

Although much that is good comes to us from men, we receive 26 it all from God through his command and ordinance. Our parents and all authorities—in short, all people placed in the position of neighbors—have received the command to do us all kinds of good. So we receive our blessings not from them, but from God through them. Creatures are only the hands, channels, and means through which God bestows all blessings. For example, he gives to the mother breasts and milk for her infant, and he gives grain and all kinds of fruits from the earth for man's nourishment—things which no creature could produce by himself. No one, therefore, should presume to 27 take or give anything except as God has commanded it. We must acknowledge everything as God's gifts and thank him for them, as this commandment requires. Therefore, this way of receiving good through God's creatures is not to be disdained, nor are we arrogantly to seek other ways and means than God has commanded, for that would be not receiving our blessings from God but seeking them from ourselves.

Let everyone, then, take care to magnify and exalt this 28 commandment above all things and not make light of it. Search and examine your own heart thoroughly and you will find whether or not it clings to God alone. Do you have the kind of heart that expects from him nothing but good, especially in distress and want, and renounces and forsakes all that is not God? Then you have the one true God. On the contrary, does your heart cling to something else, from which it hopes to receive more good and help than from God, and does it flee not to him but from him when things go wrong? Then you have an idol, another god.

Consequently, in order to show that God will not have this 29 commandment taken lightly but will strictly watch over it, he has attached to it, first, a terrible threat and, then, a beautiful, comforting promise. These should be thoroughly stressed and impressed upon young people so that they may take them to heart and remember them.

[EXPLANATION OF THE APPENDIX TO THE FIRST COMMANDMENT][6]

"For I am the Lord your God, mighty and jealous, visiting the 30 iniquity of the fathers upon the children to the third and fourth

---

[5] Luther asserted this derivation more than once. But the two words, both in old German and in Gothic, are not etymologically connected.

[6] This subtitle is found only in the Latin version.

generation of those who hate me, and showing mercy to many thousands of those who love me and keep my commandments." [7]

Although these words apply to all the commandments (as we 31 shall hear later),[8] yet they are attached precisely to this one which stands at the head of the list because it is of the utmost importance for a man to have the right head. For where the head is right, the whole life must be right, and vice versa. Learn from these words, 32 then, how angry God is with those who rely on anything but himself, and again, how kind and gracious he is to those who trust and believe him alone with their whole heart. His wrath does not abate until the fourth generation. On the other hand, his kindness and goodness 33 extend to many thousands, lest men live in security and commit themselves to luck, like brutes who think that it makes no great difference how they live. He is a God who takes vengeance upon men who 34 turn away from him, and his anger continues to the fourth generation, until they are utterly exterminated. Therefore he wills to be feared and not to be despised.

This he has witnessed in all the records of history, as Scripture 35 amply shows and as daily experience can still teach us. From the beginning he has completely rooted out all idolatry, and on that account he has destroyed both heathen and Jews; just so in our day he overthrows all false worship so that all who persist in it must ultimately perish. Even now there are proud, powerful, and rich 36 pot-bellies who, not caring whether God frowns or smiles, boast defiantly of their mammon and believe that they can withstand his wrath. But they will not succeed. Before they know it they will be wrecked, along with all they have trusted in, just as all others have perished who thought themselves to be so high and mighty.

Just because such blockheads imagine, when God refrains from 37 disturbing their security, that he is unconcerned or uninterested in such matters, he must strike and punish them so severely that he will not forget his anger down to their children's children. He intends that everyone shall be impressed and see that this is no laughing matter with him. These are also the people he means when he says, 38 "who hate me," that is, those who persist in their stubbornness and pride. They refuse to hear what is preached or spoken to them. When they are rebuked, to bring them to their senses and cause them to mend their ways before punishment descends, they become so mad and foolish that they justly merit the wrath they receive. We observe this every day in the case of bishops and princes.

---

[7] This text is virtually the same as in Luther's Bible translation at Exod. 20:5. An entirely different German rendering appears in the conclusion of his exposition of the Ten Commandments, below, 320.

[8] See below, Ten Commandments, 321, 326.

Terrible as these threats are, much mightier is the comfort in   39
the promise that assures mercy to those who cling to God alone—sheer
goodness and blessing, not only for themselves but also for their
children to a thousand and even many thousands of generations.
Certainly, if we desire all good things in time and eternity, this   40
ought to move and impel us to fix our hearts upon God with perfect
confidence since the divine Majesty comes to us with so gracious an
offer, so cordial an invitation, and so rich a promise.

Therefore let everyone be careful not to regard this as if it   41
were spoken by man. For it brings you either eternal blessing,
happiness, and salvation, or eternal wrath, misery, and woe. What
more could you ask or desire than God's gracious promise that he will
be yours with every blessing and will protect and help you in every
need? The trouble is that the world does not believe this at all,   42
and does not recognize it as God's Word. For the world sees that
those who trust God and not mammon suffer grief and want and are
opposed and attacked by the devil. They have neither money, prestige,
nor honor, and can scarcely even keep alive; meanwhile, those who
serve mammon have power, prestige, honor, wealth, and every comfort
in the eyes of the world. Accordingly, we must grasp these words,
even in the face of this apparent contradiction, and learn that they
neither lie nor deceive but will yet prove to be true.

Reflect on the past, search it out, and tell me, When men have   43
devoted all their care and diligence to scraping together great wealth
and money, what have they gained in the end? You will find that they
have wasted their effort and toil or, if they have amassed great
treasures, that these have turned to dust and vanished. They themselves have never found happiness in their wealth, nor has it ever
lasted to the third generation.[9] Examples of this you will find   44
aplenty in all histories and in the recollections of elderly and experienced people. Just ponder and heed them. Saul was a great king,   45
chosen by God, and an upright man; but once he was secure on his
throne and he let his heart depart from God, placing his confidence
in his crown and power, he inevitably perished with all that he had;
not one of his children remained.[1] David, on the other hand, was   46
a poor, despised man, hunted down and persecuted, his life nowhere
secure, yet inevitably he remained safe from Saul and became king.[2]
These words must stand and prove to be true since God cannot lie or
deceive; just leave it to the devil and the world to deceive you with

---

[9] A late Latin proverb, often quoted by Luther, declares: "Ill-gotten gains
will not last to the third generation."
[1] Cf. I Sam. 10, 15, 16, 31; II Sam. 4.
[2] Cf. I Sam. 18 to II Sam. 2.

their appearance, which indeed endures for a time but in the end is nothing! [3]

Let us therefore learn the first commandment well and realize 47 that God will tolerate no presumption and no trust in any other object; he makes no greater demand of us than a hearty trust in him for all blessings. Then we shall be on the right path and walk straight ahead, using all of God's gifts exactly as a cobbler uses his needle, awl, and thread (for work, eventually to lay them aside) or as a traveler avails himself of an inn, food, and bed (only for his temporal need). Let each person be in his station in life according to God's order, allowing none of these good things to be his lord or idol.

Let this suffice for the First Commandment. We had to explain 48 it at length since it is the most important. For, as I said before,[4] where the heart is right with God and this commandment is kept, fulfillment of all the others will follow of its own accord.

THE SECOND COMMANDMENT

"You shall not take the name of God in vain."   49

As the First Commandment has inwardly instructed the heart 50 and taught faith, so this commandment leads us outward and directs the lips and the tongue into the right relation to God. The first things that issue and emerge from the heart are words. As I have taught above how to answer the question, What it is to have a God, so you must learn to grasp simply the meaning of this and all the other commandments and apply them to yourself.

If you are asked, "How do you understand the Second Com- 51 mandment? What does it mean to misuse or take the name of God in vain?" you should answer briefly: "It is a misuse of God's name if we call upon the Lord God in any way whatsoever to support falsehood or wrong of any kind." Therefore what this commandment forbids is appealing to God's name falsely or taking his name upon our lips when our heart knows or should know that the facts are otherwise— for example, where men take oaths in court and one side lies against the other. God's name cannot be more grievously abused than for 52 purposes of falsehood and deceit. Let this stand as the plain and simple meaning of this commandment.

From this everyone can readily infer when and in how many 53 ways God's name is abused, though it is impossible to enumerate all its misuses. To discuss it briefly, misuse of the divine name occurs most obviously in worldly business and in matters involving money,

---

[3] The first Latin translator, Obsopoeus, and the German (1580) and Latin (1584) editions of the Book of Concord added a negative, thereby turning Luther's quip into a sober admonition.

[4] See above, Ten Commandments, 31.

property, and honor, whether publicly in court or in the market or elsewhere, when a person perjures himself, swearing by God's name or by his own soul. This is especially common in marriage matters when two persons secretly betroth themselves to each other and afterward deny it under oath.

The greatest abuse, however, occurs in spiritual matters, which   54 pertain to the conscience, when false preachers arise and peddle their lying nonsense as the Word of God.

See, all this is an attempt to embellish yourself with God's name   55 or to put up a good front and justify yourself, whether in ordinary worldly affairs or in sublime and difficult matters of faith and doctrine. Also to be counted among liars are blasphemers, not only the very crass ones who are well known to everyone and who disgrace God's name unabashedly (these belong in the hangman's school, not ours), but also those who publicly slander the truth and God's Word and consign it to the devil. Of this there is no need to speak further.

Let us take to heart how important this commandment is and   56 diligently shun and avoid every misuse of the holy name as the greatest sin that can be committed outwardly. For to lie and deceive is in itself a gross sin, but it is greatly aggravated when we attempt to justify and confirm it by invoking God's name and using it as a cloak to cover our shame. So from a single lie a double one results— indeed, manifold lies.

Therefore God has attached to this commandment a solemn   57 threat: "for the Lord will not hold him guiltless who takes his name in vain." This means that in no one shall a violation be condoned or left unpunished. As little as God will permit the heart that turns away from him to go unpunished, so little will he permit his name to be used to gloss over a lie. Unfortunately it is now a common   58 calamity all over the world that there are few who do not use the name of God for lies and all kinds of wickedness, just as there are few who trust in God with their whole heart.

By nature we all have this beautiful virtue that whenever we   59 commit a wrong we like to cover and gloss over our disgrace so that no one may see it or know it. No man is so arrogant as to boast before the whole world of the wickedness he has committed. We prefer to act in secret without anyone's being aware of it. Then if anyone is denounced, God and his name have to be dragged in to turn the villainy into righteousness and the disgrace into honor. This is the   60 common course of the world. Like a great deluge, it has flooded all lands. Hence we get what we deserve: plague, war, famine, fire, flood, wayward wives and children and servants, and troubles of every kind. Where else could so much misery come from? It is a great mercy that the earth still bears and sustains us.

Above all things, therefore, our young people should be strictly   61 required and trained to hold this as well as the other commandments in high regard. Whenever they transgress, we must be after them at once with the rod, confront them with the commandment, and continually impress it upon them, so that they may be brought up not merely with punishment but in the reverence and fear of God.

Now you understand what it means to take God's name in vain.   62 To repeat very briefly, it is either simply to lie and assert under his name something that is not so, or to curse, swear, conjure, and, in short, to practice wickedness of any sort.

In addition, you must also know how to use the name of God   63 aright. With the words, "You shall not take the name of God in vain," God at the same time gives us to understand that we are to use his name properly, for it has been revealed and given to us precisely for our use and benefit. Since we are forbidden here to use the   64 holy name in support of falsehood or wickedness, it follows, conversely, that we are commanded to use it in the service of truth and all that is good—for example, when we swear properly where it is necessary and required. So, also, when we teach properly; again, when we call on his name in time of need, or praise and thank him in time of prosperity, etc. All this is summarized in the command in Ps. 50:15, "Call upon me in the day of trouble: I will deliver you and you shall glorify me." All this is what we mean by calling upon his name in service of truth and using it devoutly. Thus his name is hallowed, as we pray in the Lord's Prayer.

Here you have the substance of the entire commandment   65 explained. If it is so understood, you have easily solved the question that has tormented so many teachers:[5] why swearing is forbidden in the Gospel,[6] and yet Christ, St. Paul,[7] and other saints took oaths. The explanation is briefly this: We are not to swear in support of   66 evil (that is, to a falsehood) or unnecessarily; but in support of the good and for the advantage of our neighbor we are to swear. This is a truly good work by which God is praised, truth and justice are established, falsehood is refuted, people are reconciled, obedience is rendered, and quarrels are settled. For here God himself intervenes and separates right from wrong, good from evil. If one party in   67 a dispute swears falsely, he will not escape punishment. Though it may take a long time, nothing he does will in the end succeed; everything he may gain by the false oath will slip through his fingers and will never be enjoyed. This I have seen in the case of many who broke their   68

---

[5] E.g., Augustine and Jerome. The issue had taken on new urgency with the rise of the Anabaptists.

[6] Matt. 5:33-37.

[7] Matt. 26:63f.; Gal. 1:20; II Cor. 1:23.

promise of marriage; they never enjoyed a happy hour or a healthful day thereafter, and thus they miserably perished, body, soul, and possessions.

Therefore I advise and urge, as I have before, that by means 69 of warning and threat, restraint and punishment, children be trained in due time to shun falsehood and especially to avoid calling upon God's name in its support. Where they are allowed to do as they please, no good will come of it. It is evident that the world today is more wicked than it has ever been. There is no government, no obedience, no fidelity, no faith—only perverse, unbridled men whom no teaching or punishment can help. All this is God's wrath and punishment upon such willful contempt of this commandment.

On the other hand, children should be constantly urged and 70 encouraged to honor God's name and keep it constantly upon their lips in all circumstances and experiences, for true honor to God's name consists of looking to it for all consolation and therefore calling upon it. Thus, as we have heard above, the heart by faith first gives God the honor due him and then the lips do so by confession.

This is a blessed and useful habit, and very effective against the 71 devil, who is ever around us, lying in wait to lure us into sin and shame, calamity and trouble. He hates to hear God's name and cannot long remain when it is uttered and invoked from the heart. Many a 72 terrible and shocking calamity would befall us if God did not preserve us through our calling upon his name. I have tried it myself and learned by experience that often sudden, great calamity was averted and vanished in the very moment I called upon God. To defy the devil, I say, we should always keep the holy name on our lips so that he may not be able to injure us as he is eager to do.

For this purpose it also helps to form the habit of commending 73 ourselves each day to God—our soul and body, wife, children, servants, and all that we have—for his protection against every conceivable need. Thus has originated and continued among us the custom of saying grace and returning thanks at meals and saying other prayers for both morning and evening.[8] From the same source came the 74 custom of children who cross themselves when they see or hear anything monstrous or fearful and exclaim, "Lord God, save us!" "Help, dear Lord Christ!" etc. Thus, too, if anyone meets with unexpected good fortune, however trivial, he may say, "God be praised and thanked!" "This God has bestowed upon me!" etc. Children used to be trained to fast and pray to St. Nicholas and other

[8] See the blessing before meals, the thanksgiving after meals, and the morning and evening blessings appended at the end of the Small Catechism, above.

saints, but the other practices would be more pleasing and acceptable to God than any monastic life and Carthusian holiness.[9]

With childish and playful methods like these we may bring up 75 our youth in the fear and honor of God so that the First and Second Commandments may become familiar and be constantly practiced. Then some good may take root, spring up, and bear fruit, and men may grow up of whom an entire land may be proud. This would be 76 the right way to bring up children, so long as they can be trained with kind and pleasant methods, for those who have to be forced by means of rods and blows will come to no good end; at best they will remain good only as long as the rod is on their backs.

This kind of training takes such root in their hearts that they 77 fear God more than they do rods and clubs. This I say plainly for the sake of the young, so that it may sink into their minds, for when we preach to children, we must also speak their language. Thus we have averted the misuse of the divine name and taught that its right use consists not only of words but also of practice and life. We want them to know that God is well pleased with the right use of his name and will as richly reward it, even as he will terribly punish its misuse.

THE THIRD COMMANDMENT

"You shall sanctify the holy day." 78

Our word "holy day" or "holiday" is so called from the Hebrew 79 word "Sabbath," which properly means to rest, that is, to cease from labor; hence our common expression for "stopping work" literally means "observing a holy day or holiday." [1] In the Old Testament 80 God set apart the seventh day and appointed it for rest, and he commanded it to be kept holy above all other days.[2] As far as outward observance is concerned, the commandment was given to the Jews alone. They were to abstain from hard work and to rest, so that both man and beast might be refreshed and not be exhausted by constant labor. In time, however, the Jews interpreted this commandment 81 too narrowly and grossly misused it. They slandered Christ and would not permit him to do what they themselves were in the habit of doing on that day, as we read in the Gospel[3]—as if the commandment

[9] Luther often cited the Carthusian Order (founded 1084) as an example of particularly strict asceticism and self-devised holiness.

[1] The ambiguity in the German word *Feiertag,* to which Luther refers, is discernible in the connection between the English words "holy day" and "holiday." *Feiern (feiern)* means to celebrate a festival, or simply to take time off from work. *Feierabend machen* or *heiligen Abend geben,* common expressions for "taking (or granting) time off," literally mean observing (or granting) a holy day, originally the eve of a festival.

[2] Gen. 2:3.

[3] Matt. 12:1ff.; Mark 2:23ff.; Luke 6:1ff, 13:10ff., 14:1ff.; John 5:9ff., 7:22f., 9:14ff.

could be fulfilled by refraining from manual labor of any kind. This
was not its intention, but, as we shall hear, it meant that we should
sanctify the holy day or day of rest.

Therefore, according to its literal, outward sense, this com- 82
mandment does not concern us Christians. It is an entirely external
matter, like the other ordinances of the Old Testament connected with
particular customs, persons, times, and places,[4] from all of which we
are now set free through Christ.[5]

To offer ordinary people a Christian interpretation of what 83
God requires in this commandment, we point out that we keep holy
days not for the sake of intelligent and well informed Christians, for
these have no need of them. We keep them, first, for the sake of
bodily need. Nature teaches and demands that the common people—
man-servants and maid-servants who have attended to their work and
trades the whole week long—should retire for a day to rest and be
refreshed. Secondly and most especially, we keep holy days so 84
that people may have time and opportunity, which otherwise would
not be available, to participate in public worship, that is, that they may
assemble to hear and discuss God's Word and then praise God with
song and prayer.

This, I say, is not restricted to a particular time, as it was among 85
the Jews, when it had to be precisely this or that day, for in itself no
one day is better than another. Actually, there should be worship
daily; however, since this is more than the common people can do, at
least one day in the week must be set apart for it. Since from ancient
times Sunday has been appointed for this purpose, we should not
change it. In this way a common order will prevail and no one will
create disorder by unnecessary innovation.

This, then, is the plain meaning of this commandment: Since 86
we observe holidays anyhow, we should devote their observance to
learning God's Word. The special office of this day, therefore, should
be the ministry of the Word for the sake of the young and the poor
common people. However, the observance of rest should not be so
narrow as to forbid incidental and unavoidable work.

Accordingly, when you are asked what "You shall sanctify the 87
holy day" means, answer: "It means to keep it holy." What is meant
by "keeping it holy"? Nothing else than to devote it to holy words,
holy works, holy life. In itself the day needs no sanctification, for it

---

[4] In his treatise "Against the Heavenly Prophets" (1525) Luther argued
that whatever in the Mosaic Law exceeds the natural law is strictly binding
on the Jews alone. The Mosaic Law is "the Jews' 'Saxon Code.'" France
does not observe the Saxon Code, except in so far as it agrees with its own
laws on the common ground of the natural law. Man's need for a day of
rest is a testimony of nature. Just so, Christ placed the Sabbath law under
man, Matt. 12, Mark 3 (*WA*, 18:81, 82).

[5] Cf. Col. 2:16f.

was created holy. But God wants it to be holy to you. So it becomes holy or unholy on your account, according as you spend the day in doing holy or unholy things.

How does this sanctifying take place? Not when we sit behind   88 the stove and refrain from external work, or deck ourselves with garlands and dress up in our best clothes, but, as has been said, when we occupy ourselves with God's Word and exercise ourselves in it.

Indeed, we Christians should make every day a holy day and   89 give ourselves only to holy activities—that is, occupy ourselves daily with God's Word and carry it in our hearts and on our lips. However, as we have said, since all people do not have this much time and leisure, we must set apart several hours a week for the young, and at least a day for the whole community, when we can concentrate upon such matters and deal especially with the Ten Commandments, the Creed, and the Lord's Prayer. Thus we may regulate our whole life and being according to God's Word. Wherever this practice is in   90 force, a holy day is truly kept. Where it is not, it cannot be called a Christian holy day. Non-Christians can spend a day in rest and idleness, too, and so can the whole swarm of clerics in our day who stand daily in the churches, singing and ringing bells, without sanctifying the holy day because they neither preach nor practice God's Word but teach and live contrary to it.

The Word of God is the true holy thing[6] above all holy things.   91 Indeed, it is the only one we Christians acknowledge and have. Though we had the bones of all the saints or all the holy and consecrated vestments gathered together in one heap, they could not help us in the slightest degree, for they are all dead things that can sanctify no one. But God's Word is the treasure that sanctifies all things. By it all the saints themselves have been sanctified. At whatever time God's   92 Word is taught, preached, heard, read, or pondered, there the person, the day, and the work are sanctified by it, not on account of the external work but on account of the Word which makes us all saints. Accordingly, I constantly repeat that all our life and work must be guided by God's Word if they are to be God-pleasing or holy. Where that happens the commandment is in force and is fulfilled.

Conversely, any conduct or work done apart from God's Word   93 is unholy in the sight of God, no matter how splendid and brilliant it may appear, or even if it be altogether covered with holy relics, as are the so-called spiritual estates[7] who do not know God's Word but seek holiness in their own works.

---

[6] *Heiligtum* is the word for "relic." To understand Luther's meaning, read something like this: We used to be taught to revere relics and other "holy things." But the Word of God is the true holy thing, etc.

[7] Cf. the title of Luther's treatise, "Against the Falsely So-called Spiritual Estate of the Pope and the Bishops" (1522).

Note, then, that the power and force of this commandment 94
consist not of the resting but of the sanctifying, so that this day
should have its own particular holy work. Other trades and occupations
are not properly called holy work unless the doer himself is first holy.
But here a work must be performed by which the doer himself is made
holy; this, as we have heard, takes place only through God's Word.
Places, times, persons, and the entire outward order of worship are
therefore instituted and appointed in order that God's Word may
exert its power publicly.

Since so much depends on God's Word that no holy day is 95
sanctified without it, we must realize that God insists upon a strict
observance of this commandment and will punish all who despise his
Word and refuse to hear and learn it, especially at the times appointed.

Therefore this commandment is violated not only by those who 96
grossly misuse and desecrate the holy day, like those who in their
greed or frivolity neglect to hear God's Word or lie around in taverns
dead drunk like swine, but also by that multitude of others who listen
to God's Word as they would to any other entertainment, who only
from force of habit go to hear preaching and depart again with as little
knowledge of the Word at the end of the year as at the beginning.
It used to be thought that Sunday had been properly hallowed if 97
one heard a Mass or the reading of the Gospel; no one asked about
God's Word, and no one taught it either. Now that we have God's
Word, we still fail to remove the abuse of the holy day, for we permit
ourselves to be preached to and admonished but we listen without
serious concern.

Remember, then, that you must be concerned not only about 98
hearing the Word but also about learning and retaining it. Do not
regard it as an optional or unimportant matter. It is the commandment
of God, and he will require of you an accounting of how you have
heard and learned and honored his Word.

In the same way those conceited fellows should be chastised 99
who, after hearing a sermon or two, become sick and tired of it and
feel that they know it all and need no more instruction. This is
precisely the sin that used to be classed among the mortal sins and was
called *acidia*[8]—that is, indolence or satiety—a malignant, pernicious
plague with which the devil bewitches and befuddles the hearts of many
so that he may take us by surprise and stealthily take the Word of God
away from us.

Let me tell you this. Even though you know the Word perfectly 100
and have already mastered everything, still you are daily under the
dominion of the devil, who neither day nor night relaxes his effort to
steal upon you unawares and to kindle in your heart unbelief and

---

[8] The term *acedia* (or *acidia*) comes from Aristotle's Ethics, Book IV.

wicked thoughts against all these commandments. Therefore you must
continually keep God's Word in your heart, on your lips, and in your
ears. For where the heart stands idle and the Word is not heard, the
devil breaks in and does his damage before we realize it. On the | 101
other hand, when we seriously ponder the Word, hear it, and put it
to use, such is its power that it never departs without fruit. It always
awakens new understanding, new pleasure, and a new spirit of devotion,
and it constantly cleanses the heart and its meditations. For these
words are not idle or dead, but effective and living. Even if no | 102
other interest or need drove us to the Word, yet everyone should be
spurred on by the realization that in this way the devil is cast out and
put to flight, this commandment is fulfilled, and God is more pleased
than by any work of hypocrisy, however brilliant.

THE FOURTH COMMANDMENT

Thus far we have learned the first three commandments, which | 103
are directed toward God. First, we should trust, fear, and love him
with our whole heart all the days of our lives. Secondly, we should not
misuse his holy name in support of lies or any evil purpose whatsoever,
but use it for the praise of God and the benefit and salvation of our
neighbor and ourselves. Thirdly, on holy days or days of rest we
should diligently devote ourselves to God's Word so that all our
conduct and life may be regulated by it. Now follow the other seven,
which relate to our neighbor. Among these the first and greatest is:

"You shall honor your father and mother." | 104

To fatherhood and motherhood God has given the special | 105
distinction, above all estates that are beneath it, that he commands us
not simply to love our parents but also to honor them. With respect
to brothers, sisters, and neighbors in general he commands nothing
higher than that we love them. Thus he distinguishes father and
mother above all other persons on earth, and places them next to
himself. For it is a much greater thing to honor than to love. | 106
Honor includes not only love but also deference, humility, and
modesty, directed (so to speak) toward a majesty hidden within them.
It requires us not only to address them affectionately and | 107
reverently, but above all to show by our actions, both of heart and of
body, that we respect them very highly and that next to God we give
them the very highest place. For anyone whom we are whole-heartedly
to honor, we must truly regard as high and great.

Young people must therefore be taught to revere their parents | 108
as God's representatives, and to remember that, however lowly, poor,
feeble, and eccentric they may be, they are their own father and
mother, given them by God. They are not to be deprived of their
honor because of their ways or their failings. Therefore, we are not
to think of their persons, whatever they are, but of the will of God,

who has created and ordained them to be our parents. In other respects, indeed, we are all equal in the sight of God, but among ourselves there must be this sort of inequality and proper distinctions. God therefore commands you to be careful to obey me as your father and to acknowledge my authority.

First, then, learn what this commandment requires concerning 109 honor to parents. You are to esteem and prize them as the most precious treasure on earth. In your words you are to behave 110 respectfully toward them, and not address them discourteously, critically, and censoriously, but submit to them and hold your tongue, even if they go too far. You are also to honor them by your 111 actions (that is, with your body and possessions), serving them, helping them, and caring for them when they are old, sick, feeble, or poor; all this you should do not only cheerfully, but with humility and reverence, as in God's sight. He who has the right attitude toward his parents will not allow them to suffer want or hunger, but will place them above himself and at his side and will share with them all he has to the best of his ability.

In the second place, notice what a great, good, and holy work 112 is here assigned to children. Alas, it is utterly despised and brushed aside, and no one recognizes it as God's command or as a holy, divine word and precept. For if we had regarded it as such, it would have been apparent to all that they who lived according to these words must also be holy men. Then there would have been no need to institute monasticism or "spiritual estates." Every child would have remained faithful to this commandment and would have been able to set his conscience right toward God, saying: "If I am to do good and holy works, I know of none better than to show all honor and obedience to my parents, since God himself has commanded it. What God commands must be much nobler than anything we 113 ourselves may devise. And because there is no greater or better teacher to be found than God, there can also be no better teaching than his. Now, he amply teaches what we should do if we wish to perform truly good works, and by commanding them he shows that he is well pleased with them. So, if this is God's command, and it embodies his highest wisdom, then I shall never improve upon it."

In this way, you see, we should have had godly children, 114 properly taught, and reared in true blessedness; they would have remained at home in obedience and service to their parents, and we should have had an object lesson in goodness and happiness. However, men did not feel obliged to set forth God's commandment in its full glory. They were able to ignore it and skip lightly over it, and so children could not lay it to heart; they simply gaped in astonishment at all the arrangements we have devised without ever asking God's approval.

For the love of God, therefore. let us at last teach our young 115
people to banish all other things from sight and give first place to this
commandment. If they wish to serve God with truly good works, they
must do what is pleasing to their fathers and mothers, or to those
who have parental authority over them. Every child who knows and
does this has, in the first place, the great comfort of being able
joyfully to boast in the face of all who are occupied with works of
their own choice: "See, this work is well pleasing to my God in
heaven; this I know for certain." Let them all come forward 116
and boast of their many great, laborious, and difficult works; we shall
see whether they can produce a single work that is greater and nobler
than obedience to father and mother, which God has appointed and
commanded next to obedience to his own majesty. If God's Word
and will are placed first and observed, nothing ought to be considered
more important than the will and word of our parents, provided that
these, too, are subordinated to obedience toward God and are not set
into opposition to the preceding commandments.

You should rejoice heartily and thank God that he has chosen 117
and fitted you to perform a task so precious and pleasing to him.
Even though it seems very trivial and contemptible, make sure that you
regard it as great and precious, not on account of your worthiness but
because it has its place within that jewel and holy treasure, the Word
and commandment of God. O how great a price all the 118
Carthusian monks and nuns[9] would pay if in the exercise of their
religion they could bring before God a single work done in accordance
with his commandment and could say with a joyful heart in his
presence, "Now I know that this work is well pleasing to Thee!"
What will become of these poor wretched people when, standing before
God and the whole world, they shall blush with shame before a little
child that has lived according to this commandment and confess that
with the merits of their whole lives they are not worthy to offer him
a cup of water? It serves them right for their devilish perversity 119
in trampling God's commandment under foot that they must torture
themselves in vain with their self-devised works[1] and meanwhile have
only scorn and trouble for their reward.

Should not the heart leap and melt with joy when it can go to 120
work and do what is commanded, saying, "Lo, this is better than the
holiness of all the Carthusians, even though they kill themselves with
fasting and pray on their knees without ceasing"? Hence you have a
sure text and a divine testimony that God has commanded this;

---

[9] Here and elsewhere the translator of the Latin version, Obsopoeus,
altered "Carthusians" into "Carmelites," a hermit order founded *ca.* 1180
on Mt. Carmel in Palestine, later transformed into a mendicant order.

[1] Self-appointed works in contrast to God's commands—for example, the
injunction to strict silence, avoidance of meat, extreme vigils, etc.

concerning the other things he has commanded not a word. This is the plight and the miserable blindness of the world that no one believes this; so thoroughly has the devil bewitched us with the false holiness and glamor of our own works.

Therefore, I repeat, I should be very glad if we were to open |21| our eyes and ears and take this to heart so that we may not again be led astray from the pure Word of God to the lying vanities of the devil. Then all would be well; parents would have more happiness, love, kindness, and harmony in their houses, and children would win their parents' hearts completely. On the other hand, when they |22| are obstinate and never do their duty until a rod is laid on their backs, they anger both God and their parents. Thus they deprive themselves of this treasure and joy of conscience and lay up for themselves nothing but misfortune. That is the way things go in the world |23| now, as everyone complains. Both young and old are altogether wayward and unruly; they have no sense of modesty or honor; they do nothing until they are driven with blows; and they defame and depreciate one another behind their backs in any way they can. God therefore punishes them so that they sink into all kinds of trouble and misery. Neither can parents, as a rule, do very much; one |24| fool trains another, and as they have lived, so live their children after them.

This, I say, should be the first and strongest reason impelling |25| us to keep this commandment. If we had no father and mother, we should wish, on account of the commandments, that God would set up a block or a stone which we might call father and mother. How much more, when he has given us living parents, should we be happy to show them honor and obedience. For we know that it is highly pleasing to the divine Majesty and all the angels, that it vexes all devils, and, besides, that it is the greatest work that we can do, next to the sublime worship of God described in the previous commandments. Even |26| almsgiving and all other works for our neighbor are not equal to this. For God has exalted this estate of parents above all others; indeed, he has appointed it to be his representative on earth. This will and pleasure of God ought to provide us sufficient reason and incentive to do cheerfully and gladly whatever we can.

Besides this, it is our duty before the world to show gratitude |27| for the kindness and for all the good things we have received from our parents. But here again the devil rules in the world; children |28| forget their parents, as we all forget God, and no one takes thought how God feeds, guards, and protects us and how many blessings of body and soul he bestows upon us. Especially when an evil hour comes do we rage and grumble impatiently and forget all the blessings we have received throughout our life. Just so we act toward our

parents, and there is no child that recognizes and considers this, unless
he is led to it by the Holy Spirit.

The perversity of the world God knows very well. By means of |29
commandments, therefore, he reminds and impels everyone to consider
what his parents have done for him. Then everybody recognizes that
he has received his body and life from them and that he has been
nourished and nurtured by them when otherwise he would have
perished a hundred times in his own filth. The wise men of old |30
were right when they said, "God, parents, and teachers can never be
sufficiently thanked and repaid." [2] He who views the matter in this
light will, without compulsion, give all honor to his parents and esteem
them as those through whom God has given him all blessings.

Over and above all this, another strong incentive for us to |3|
keep this commandment is that God has attached to it a lovely
promise, "That you may have long life in the land where you dwell."
Here you see how important God considers this commandment. |32
He declares that it is not only an object of pleasure and delight to
himself, but also an instrument intended for our greatest welfare, to
lead us to a quiet, pleasant, and blessed life. St. Paul also highly |33
exalts and praises this commandment, saying in Eph. 6:2, 3, "This is
the first commandment with a promise: that it may be well with you
and that you may live long on the earth." Although the other
commandments also have a promise implied, yet in none is it so
plainly and explicitly stated.

This, then, is the fruit and the reward, that whoever keeps |34
this commandment will enjoy good days, happiness, and prosperity.
On the other hand, the penalty for him who disobeys it is that he
will perish sooner and never be happy in life. For, in the Scriptures,
to have long life means not merely to grow old but to have everything
that pertains to long life—health, wife and child, livelihood, peace,
good government, etc., without which this life can neither be heartily
enjoyed nor long endure. If you are unwilling to obey father and |35
mother or to submit to them, then obey the hangman; and if you will
not obey him, then obey the grim reaper,[3] Death! This, in short, |36
is the way God will have it: render him obedience and love and service,
and he will reward you abundantly with every blessing; on the other
hand, if you provoke him to anger, he will send upon you both death
and the hangman.

---

[2] Cf. *WA*, 30[II]:579: "A diligent, upright schoolteacher or master, or
anyone who faithfully trains and teaches boys, can never be sufficiently
repaid, as the pagan Aristotle says."

[3] Luther often used the word *Streckebein,* primarily a Low German
expression for death. A parallel word is *Streckefuss.* A seventeenth century
explanation is that in mortal illness the legs give out before the head, i.e., the
dying man is stretched out on his bed. Obsopoeus translated the word with
carnifex, executioner.

Why do we have so many criminals who must daily be hanged,   137
beheaded, or broken on the wheel if not because of disobedience?
They will not allow themselves to be brought up in kindness; consequently, by the punishment of God they bring upon themselves the
misfortune and grief that we behold, for it seldom happens that such
wicked people die a natural and timely death.

The godly and the obedient, however, are blessed. They live long
in peace and quietness. They see their children's children, as we said
above, "to the third and fourth generation." Again, as we know   138
from experience, where there are fine old families who prosper and
have many children, it is certainly because some of them were brought
up well and revered their parents. On the other hand, it is written of
the wicked in Ps. 109:13, "May his posterity be cut off: and may
their name be cut off in one generation." Learn well, then, how   139
important God considers obedience, since he so highly exalts it, so
greatly delights in it, so richly rewards it, and besides is so strict about
punishing those who transgress it.

All this I say that it may be thoroughly impressed upon the   140
young people, for no one will believe how necessary is this commandment, which in the past was neither heeded nor taught under the
papacy. These are plain and simple words, and everyone thinks he
already knows them well. So he passes over them lightly, fastens
his attention on other things, and fails to perceive and believe how
angry he makes God when he neglects this commandment, and how
precious and acceptable a work he does when he observes it.

In connection with this commandment there is more to be said   141
about the various kinds of obedience due to our superiors, persons
whose duty it is to command and to govern. Out of the authority
of parents all other authority is derived and developed. Where a
father is unable by himself to bring up his child, he calls upon a
schoolmaster to teach him; if he is too weak, he enlists the help
of his friends and neighbors; if he passes away, he confers and
delegates his authority and responsibility to others appointed for the
purpose. Likewise he must have domestics (man-servants and   142
maid-servants) under him to manage the household. Thus all who are
called masters stand in the place of parents and derive from them
their power and authority to govern. In the Scriptures they are all
called fathers because in their responsibility they act in the capacity
of fathers and ought to have fatherly hearts toward their people. So
from ancient times the Romans and other peoples called the masters
and mistresses of the household *patres et matres familias* (that is,
house-fathers and house-mothers). Again, their princes and overlords
were called *patres patriae*[4] (that is, fathers of the country) to the

---

[4] Cicero received this title after exposing the conspiracy of Catiline. In
later times it became a part of the Roman emperor's official title.

great shame of us would-be Christians who do not speak of our rulers
in the same way, or at least do not treat and honor them as such.

What a child owes to father and mother, the entire household 143
owes them likewise. Therefore man-servants and maid-servants should
take care not only to obey their masters and mistresses, but also to
honor them as their own parents and do everything that they know is
expected of them, not from compulsion and reluctantly but gladly and
cheerfully; and they should do it for the reason just mentioned, that it
is God's commandment and is more pleasing to him than all other
works. They ought even to be willing to pay for the privilege of 144
service and be glad to acquire masters and mistresses in order to have
such joyful consciences and know how to do truly golden works.
These works in the past have been neglected and despised; instead,
everybody ran in the devil's name into monasteries, on pilgrimages,
and after indulgences, to their own hurt and with a bad conscience.

If this truth could be impressed upon the poor people, a 145
servant girl would dance for joy and praise and thank God; and with
her careful work, for which she receives sustenance and wages, she
would gain a treasure such as all who pass for the greatest saints
do not have. Is it not a wonderful thing to be able to boast to
yourself, "If I do my daily housework faithfully, that is better than the
holiness and austere life of all the monks"? You have the promise, 146
moreover, that you will prosper and fare well in everything. How
can you lead a more blessed or holy life, as far as your works are
concerned? In the sight of God it is really faith that makes a 147
person holy; faith alone serves him, while our works serve the people.
Here you have everything that is good—shelter and protection 148
in the Lord and, what is more, a joyful conscience and a gracious God
who will reward you a hundredfold. You are a true nobleman if you
are upright and obedient. If you are not, you will have nothing but
the wrath and displeasure of God; there will be no peace in your
heart, and eventually you will have all kinds of trouble and misfortune.

Whoever will not be moved by this, and who will not be 149
inclined to godliness, we deliver to the hangman and the grim reaper.
Therefore, let everyone who can take advice remember that God is
not to be taken lightly. God speaks to you and demands obedience.
If you obey him you are his dear child; if you despise this commandment, then take shame, misery, and grief for your reward.

The same may be said of obedience to the civil government, 150
which, as we have said, is to be classed with the estate of fatherhood,
the most comprehensive of all relations. In this case a man is father
not of a single family, but of as many people as he has inhabitants,
citizens, or subjects. Through civil rulers, as through our own parents,
God gives us food, house and home, protection and security. Therefore,
since they bear this name and title with all honor as their chief glory,

it is our duty to honor and magnify them as the most precious treasure and jewel on earth.

He who is obedient, willing, ready to serve, and cheerfully |51| gives honor where it is due, knows that he pleases God and receives joy and happiness for his reward. On the other hand, if he will not do so in love, but despises or rebelliously resists authority, let him know that he shall have no favor or blessing from God. Where he counts on gaining a gulden[5] by his unfaithfulness, he will lose ten elsewhere. Or he will fall victim to the hangman, or perish through war, pestilence, or famine, or his children will turn out badly; servants, neighbors, or strangers and tyrants will inflict injury, injustice, and violence upon him. What we seek and deserve, then, is paid back to us in retaliation.

If we ever let ourselves be persuaded that works of obedience |52| are so pleasing to God and have so rich a reward, we shall be simply overwhelmed with our blessings and we shall have all that our hearts desire. But God's Word and commandment are despised, as if they came from some loutish peddler. Let us see, though, whether you are the man to defy him. How difficult do you think it will be for him to pay you back? You will live much better with God's favor, |53| peace, and blessing than you will with disfavor and misfortune. Why, do you think, is the world now so full of unfaithfulness, |54| shame, misery, and murder? It is because everyone wishes to be his own master, be free from all authority, care nothing for anyone, and do whatever he pleases. So God punishes one knave by means of another. When you defraud or despise your master, another person comes along and treats you likewise. Indeed, in your own household you must suffer ten times as much wrong from your own wife, children, or servants.

Of course, we keenly feel our misfortune, and we grumble and |55| complain of unfaithfulness, violence, and injustice; but we are unwilling to see that we ourselves are knaves who have roundly deserved punishment and that we are not one bit improved by it. We spurn favor and happiness; therefore, it is only fair that we have nothing but unhappiness without mercy. Somewhere on earth there must |56| still be some godly people, or else God would not grant us so many blessings! If it depended on our merits, we would not have a penny[6] in the house or a straw in the field. All this I have been obliged |57| to set forth with such a profusion of words in the hope that someone may take it to heart, so that we may be delivered from the blindness and misery in which we are so deeply sunk and may rightly understand

---

[5] The gulden was originally a large gold coin, later also silver, the equivalent of a florin.

[6] In popular expressions the heller, or penny, represented extreme insignificance in contrast with the groschen and other coins.

the Word and will of God and sincerely accept it. From God's Word we could learn how to obtain an abundance of joy, happiness, and salvation, both here and in eternity.

Thus we have three kinds of fathers presented in this com- 158 mandment: fathers by blood, fathers of a household, and fathers of the nation. Besides these, there are also spiritual fathers—not like those in the papacy who applied this title to themselves but performed no fatherly office. For the name spiritual father belongs only to those who govern and guide us by the Word of God. St. Paul boasts 159 that he is a father in I Cor. 4:15, where he says, "I became your father in Christ Jesus through the Gospel." Since such persons are 160 fathers, they are entitled to honor, even above all others. But they very seldom receive it, for the world's way of honoring them is to harry them out of the country and grudge them as much as a piece of bread. In short, as St. Paul says, they must be "the refuse of the world, and every man's offscouring." [7]

Yet there is need to impress upon the common people that 161 they who would bear the name of Christians owe it to God to show "double honor" [8] to those who watch over their souls and to treat them well and make provision for them. God will adequately recompense those who do so and will not let them suffer want. But here everybody resists and rebels; all are afraid that their 162 bellies will suffer, and therefore they cannot now support one good preacher although in the past they filled ten fat paunches. For 163 this we deserve to have God deprive us of his Word and his blessings and once again allow preachers of lies[9] to arise and lead us to the devil—and wring sweat and blood out of us besides.

Those who keep their eyes on God's will and commandment, 164 however, have the promise that they will be richly rewarded for all they contribute to their temporal and spiritual fathers, and for the honor they render them. Not only shall they have bread, clothing, and money for a year or two, but long life, sustenance, and peace, and afterwards abundance and blessedness forever. Do your duty, 165 then, and leave it to God how he will support you and provide for all your wants. Since he has promised it, and has never yet lied, he will not lie to you either.

This ought to encourage us and make our hearts so melt for 166 joy and love toward those to whom we owe honor that we lift our hands in joyful thanks to God for giving us such promises. We ought to be willing to run to the ends of the world to obtain them. For the

[7] I Cor. 4:13.

[8] I Tim. 5:17.

[9] "Preachers of lies" (cf. Mic. 2:11) was a favorite epithet in the sixteenth century.

combined efforts of the whole world cannot add an hour to our life or raise from the earth a single grain of wheat for us. But God can and will give you everything abundantly, according to your heart's desire. He who despises and disdains this is not worthy to hear a word from God.

More than enough has now been said to those to whom this commandment applies.

In addition, it would be well to preach to parents on the nature 167 of their office, how they should treat those committed to their authority. Although the duty of superiors is not explicitly stated in the Ten Commandments, it is frequently dealt with in many other passages of Scripture, and God intends it to be included in this commandment in which he speaks of father and mother. God 168 does not want to have knaves or tyrants in this office and responsibility; nor does he assign them this honor (that is, power and authority to govern) merely to receive homage. Parents should consider that they owe obedience to God, and that, above all, they should earnestly and faithfully discharge the duties of their office, not only to provide for the material support of their children, servants, subjects, etc., but especially to bring them up to the praise and honor of God. Therefore do not imagine that the parental office is a matter of 169 your pleasure and whim. It is a strict commandment and injunction of God, who holds you accountable for it.

The trouble is that no one perceives or heeds this. Everybody 170 acts as if God gave us children for our pleasure and amusement, gave us servants merely to put them to work like cows or asses, and gave us subjects to treat them as we please, as if it were no concern of ours what they learn or how they live. No one is willing to see that 171 this is the command of the divine Majesty, who will solemnly call us to account and punish us for its neglect, nor is it recognized how very necessary it is to devote serious attention to the young. If we 172 want qualified and capable men for both civil and spiritual leadership, we must spare no effort, time, and expense in teaching and educating our children to serve God and mankind. We must not think only of amassing money and property for them. God can provide for 173 them and make them rich without our help, as indeed he does daily. But he has given and entrusted children to us with the command that we train and govern them according to his will; otherwise God would have no need of father and mother. Therefore let everybody 174 know that it is his chief duty, on pain of losing divine grace, to bring up his children in the fear and knowledge of God, and if they are gifted to give them opportunity to learn and study so that they may be of service wherever they are needed.

If this were done, God would richly bless us and give us grace 175 so that men might be trained who would be a benefit to the nation and the people. We would also have soundly instructed citizens, virtuous and home-loving wives who would faithfully bring up their children and servants to be godly. Think what deadly harm you 176 do when you are negligent in this respect and fail to bring up your children to usefulness and piety. You bring upon yourself sin and wrath, thus earning hell by the way you have reared your own children, no matter how devout and holy you may be in other respects. Because this commandment is disregarded, God terribly punishes 177 the world; hence there is no longer any civil order, peace, or respect for authority. We all complain about this state of things, but we do not see that it is our own fault. Because of the way we train them, we have unruly and disobedient subjects.

This is enough to serve as a warning; a more extensive 178 explanation will have to await another occasion.[1]

THE FIFTH COMMANDMENT

"You shall not kill."   179

We have now dealt with both the spiritual and the civil govern- 180 ment, that is, divine and paternal authority and obedience. In this commandment we leave our own house and go out among our neighbors to learn how we should conduct ourselves individually toward our fellow men. Therefore neither God nor the government is included in this commandment, yet their right to take human life is not abrogated. God has delegated his authority of punishing evil-doers to civil 181 magistrates in place of parents; in early times, as we read in Moses,[2] parents had to bring their own children to judgment and sentence them to death. Therefore what is forbidden here applies to private individuals, not to governments.

This commandment is simple enough. We hear it explained 182 every year in the Gospel, Matthew 5,[3] where Christ himself explains and summarizes it: We must not kill, either by hand, heart, or word, by signs or gestures, or by aiding and abetting. It forbids anger except, as we have said, to persons who occupy the place of God, that is, parents and rulers. Anger, reproof, and punishment are the prerogatives of God and his representatives, and they are to be exercised upon those who transgress this and the other commandments.

The occasion and need for this commandment is that, as God 183 well knows, the world is evil and this life is full of misery. He has therefore placed this and the other commandments as a boundary between good and evil. There are many offenses against this command-

---

[1] Soon after this Luther wrote his "Sermon on Keeping Children in School" (1530).

[2] Deut. 21:18-20.

[3] Matt. 5:20-26 is the Gospel for the sixth Sunday after Trinity. We have 16 sermons of Luther on this text.

ment, as there are against all the others. We must live among many people who do us harm, and so we have reason to be at enmity with them. For instance, a neighbor, envious that you have received |184 from God a better house and estate or greater wealth and good fortune than he, gives vent to his irritation and envy by speaking ill of you.

Thus by the devil's prompting you acquire many enemies who begrudge you even the least good, whether physical or spiritual. When we see such people, our hearts in turn rage and we are ready to shed blood and take revenge. Then follow cursing and blows, and eventually calamity and murder. Here God, like a kind father, |185 steps in and intervenes to get the quarrel settled for the safety of all concerned. Briefly, he wishes to have all people defended, delivered, and protected from the wickedness and violence of others, and he has set up this commandment as a wall, fortress, and refuge about our neighbor so that no one may do him bodily harm or injury.

What this commandment teaches, then, is that no one should |186 harm another for any evil deed, no matter how much he deserves it. Not only is murder forbidden, but also everything that may lead to murder. Many persons, though they may not actually commit murder, nevertheless call down curses and imprecations upon their enemy's head, which, if they came true, would soon put an end to him. This spirit or revenge clings to every one of us, and it is common |187 knowledge that no one willingly suffers injury from another. Therefore God wishes to remove the root and source of this bitterness toward our neighbor. He wants us to keep this commandment ever before our eyes as a mirror in which to see ourselves, so that we may be attentive to his will and with hearty confidence and prayer commit to him whatever wrong we suffer. Then we shall be content to let our enemies rave and rage and do their worst. Thus we may learn to calm our anger and have a patient, gentle heart, especially toward those who have given us occasion for anger, namely, our enemies.

Briefly, then, to impress it unmistakably upon the common |188 people, the import of the commandment against killing is this: In the first place, we should not harm anyone. This means, first, by hand or by deed; next, we should not use our tongue to advocate or advise harming anyone; again, we should neither use nor sanction any means or methods whereby anyone may be harmed; finally, our heart should harbor no hostility or malice toward anyone in a spirit of anger and hatred. Thus you should be blameless toward all people in body and soul, especially toward him who wishes or does you evil. For to do evil to somebody who desires and does you good is not human but devilish.

In the second place, this commandment is violated not only |189 when a person actually does evil, but also when he fails to do good to his neighbor, or, though he has the opportunity, fails to prevent, protect,

and save him from suffering bodily harm or injury. If you send   190
a person away naked when you could clothe him, you have let him
freeze to death. If you see anyone suffer hunger and do not feed him,
you have let him starve. Likewise, if you see anyone condemned[4] to
death or in similar peril and do not save him although you know ways
and means to do so, you have killed him. It will do you no good to
plead that you did not contribute to his death by word or deed, for
you have withheld your love from him and robbed him of the service
by which his life might have been saved.

Therefore God rightly calls all persons murderers who do not   191
offer counsel and aid to men in need and in peril of body and life. He
will pass a most terrible sentence upon them in the day of judgment,
as Christ himself declares. He will say: "I was hungry and thirsty
and you gave me no food or drink, I was a stranger, and you did not
welcome me, I was naked and you did not clothe me, I was sick and in
prison, and you did not visit me." [5] That is to say, "You would have
permitted me and my followers to die of hunger, thirst, and cold, to be
torn to pieces by wild beasts, to rot in prison or perish from want."

What else is this but to reproach such persons as murderers and   192
bloodhounds? For although you have not actually committed all these
crimes, as far as you were concerned you have nevertheless permitted
your neighbor to languish and perish in his misfortune.

It is just as if I saw someone wearily struggling in deep water, or
fallen into a fire, and could extend him my hand to pull him out and
save him, and yet I did not do it. How would I appear before all the
world in any other light than as a murderer and a scoundrel?

Therefore it is God's real intention that we should allow no   193
man to suffer harm, but show to everyone all kindness and love.
And this kindness is directed, as I said, especially toward our   194
enemies. To show kindness to our friends is but an ordinary heathen
virtue, as Christ says in Matthew 5:46, 47.

Here again we have God's Word by which he wants to   195
encourage and urge us to true, noble, exalted deeds, such as gentleness,
patience, and, in short, love and kindness toward our enemies. He
always wants to remind us to think back to the First Commandment,
that he is our God; that is, he wishes to help and protect us, so that he
may subdue our desire for revenge.

If this could be thoroughly impressed on people's minds, we   196
would have our hands full of good works to do. But this would   197
be no preaching for monks. It would too greatly undermine the
"spiritual estate" and infringe upon the holiness of the Carthusians. It
would be practically the same as forbidding their good works and

---

[4] Variant reading: innocently condemned.
[5] Matt. 25:42, 43.

emptying the monasteries. For in this teaching the ordinary Christian life would be considered just as acceptable, and even more so. Everybody would see how the monks mock and mislead the world with a false, hypocritical show of holiness, while they have thrown this and the other commandments to the winds, regarding them as unnecessary, as if they were not commandments but mere counsels.[6] Moreover, they have shamelessly boasted and bragged of their hypocritical calling and works as "the most perfect life," so that they might live a nice, soft life without the cross and suffering. This is why they fled to the monasteries, so that they might not have to suffer wrong from anyone or do anyone any good. Know, however, that it is the works   198 commanded by God's Word which are the true, holy, and divine works in which he rejoices with all the angels. In contrast to them all human holiness is only stench and filth, and it merits nothing but wrath and damnation.

THE SIXTH COMMANDMENT

"You shall not commit adultery."   199

The following commandments are easily understood from the   200 preceding one. They all teach us to guard against harming our neighbor in any way. They are admirably arranged. First they deal with our neighbor's person. Then they proceed to the person nearest and dearest to him, namely, his wife, who is one flesh and blood with him.[7] In no possession of his can we inflict a greater injury upon him. Therefore, it is explicitly forbidden here to dishonor his wife. Adultery is particularly mentioned because among the Jewish   201 people marriage was obligatory. Youths were married at the earliest age possible. The state of virginity was not commended, neither were public prostitution and lewdness tolerated as they are now. Accordingly adultery was the most common form of unchastity among them.

Inasmuch as there is a shameful mess and cesspool of all   202 kinds of vice and lewdness among us, this commandment applies to every form of unchastity, however it is called. Not only is the external act forbidden, but also every kind of cause, motive, and means. Your heart, your lips, and your whole body are to be chaste and to afford no occasion, aid, or encouragement to unchastity. Moreover,   203 you are to defend, protect, and rescue your neighbor whenever he is in danger or need, and on the contrary to aid and assist him so that he may retain his honor. Whenever you fail to do this (though you   204 could prevent a wrong) or wink at it as if it were no concern of yours,

---

[6] Luther here is making a sarcastic play on the Roman Catholic distinction between "commandments" and "(evangelical) counsels" according to which all men are unconditionally obligated to keep the "commandments," but a voluntary observance of the "counsels" brings special grace while their non-observance is no sin.

[7] Cf. Gen. 2:24.

you are just as guilty as the culprit himself. In short, everyone   205
is required both to live chastely himself and to help his neighbor do
the same. Thus God by his commandment wants every husband or
wife guarded and protected from any trespass.

Inasmuch as this commandment is concerned specifically with   206
the estate of marriage and gives occasion to speak of it, let us
carefully note, first, how highly God honors and glorifies the married
life, sanctioning and protecting it by his commandment. He sanctioned
it above in the fourth commandment, "You shall honor father and
mother"; but here, as I said, he has secured it and protected it.
Therefore he also wishes us to honor, maintain, and cherish it   207
as a divine and blessed estate. Significantly he established it as the
first of all institutions, and he created man and woman differently
(as is evident) not for lewdness but to be true to each other, be
fruitful, beget children, and support and bring them up to the glory
of God.

God has therefore most richly blessed this estate above all   208
others and, in addition, has supplied and endowed it with everything
in the world in order that this estate might be provided for richly and
adequately. Married life is no matter for jest or idle curiosity, but
it is a glorious institution and an object of God's serious concern.
For it is of the highest importance to him that persons be brought up
to serve the world, promote knowledge of God, godly living, and all
virtues, and fight against wickedness and the devil.

Therefore I have always taught that we should not despise or   209
disdain marriage, as the blind world and the false clergy do, but view
it in the light of God's Word, by which it is adorned and sanctified.
It is not an estate to be placed on a level with the others; it precedes
and surpasses them all, whether those of emperor, princes, bishops, or
anyone else. Important as the spiritual and civil estates are, these
must humble themselves and allow all people to enter the estate of
marriage, as we shall hear. It is not an exceptional estate, but   210
the most universal and the noblest, pervading all Christendom and
even extending throughout all the world.

In the second place, remember that it is not only an honorable   211
estate but also a necessary one, and it is solemnly commanded by God
that in general men and women in all conditions, who have been
created for it, shall be found in this estate. Yet there are some
(although few) exceptions whom God has especially exempted—some
who are unsuited for married life and others whom he has released by
a high supernatural gift so that they can maintain chastity outside of
marriage. Where nature has its way, as God implanted it, it is not   212
possible to remain chaste outside of marriage; for flesh and blood
remain flesh and blood, and the natural inclinations and stimulations
have their way without let or hindrance, as everyone's observation and

experience testify. Therefore, to make it easier for man to avoid unchastity in some measure, God has established marriage, so that everyone may have his allotted portion and be satisfied with it— although here, too, God's grace is still required to keep the heart pure.

From this you see how the papal rabble, priests, monks, and   213 nuns resist God's order and commandment when they despise and forbid marriage, and boast and vow that they will maintain perpetual chastity while they deceive the common people with lying words and wrong impressions. For no one has so little love and inclination   214 for chastity as those who under the guise of great sanctity avoid marriage and either indulge in open and shameless fornication or secretly do even worse—things too evil to mention, as unfortunately has been only too well proved. In short, even though they   215 abstain from the act, yet their hearts remain so full of unchaste thoughts and evil desires that they suffer incessant ragings of secret passion, which can be avoided in married life. Therefore all vows   216 of chastity apart from marriage are condemned and annulled by this commandment; indeed, all poor, captive consciences deceived by their monastic vows are even commanded to forsake their unchaste existence and enter the married life. Even granting that the monastic life is godly, yet it is not in their power to maintain chastity, and if they remain they will inevitably sin more and more against this commandment.

I say these things in order that our young people may be led   217 to acquire a love for married life and know that it is a blessed and God-pleasing estate. Thus it may in due time regain its proper honor, and there may be less of the filthy, dissolute, disorderly conduct which now is so rampant everywhere in public prostitution and other shameful vices resulting from contempt of married life. Therefore   218 parents and magistrates have the duty of so supervising youth that they will be brought up to decency and respect for authority and, when they are grown, will be married honorably in the fear of God. Then God will add his blessing and grace so that men may have joy and happiness in their married life.

Let it be said in conclusion that this commandment requires   219 everyone not only to live chastely in thought, word, and deed in his particular situation (that is, especially in the estate of marriage), but also to love and cherish the wife or husband whom God has given. For marital chastity it is above all things essential that husband and wife live together in love and harmony, cherishing each other whole-heartedly and with perfect fidelity. This is one of the chief ways to make chastity attractive and desirable. Under such conditions chastity always follows spontaneously without any command. This is why   220 St. Paul so urgently admonishes husbands and wives to love and honor

each other.[8] Here you have another precious good work—indeed,   221
many and great works—which you can joyfully set over against all
"spiritual estates" that are chosen without God's Word and
commandment.

THE SEVENTH COMMANDMENT

"You shall not steal."   222

Next to our own own person and our spouse, our temporal   223
property is dearest to us. This, too, God wants to have protected. He
has forbidden us to rob or pilfer the possessions of our neighbor.
For to steal is nothing else than to acquire another's property by   224
unjust means. In a few words, this includes taking advantage of our
neighbor in any sort of dealing that results in loss to him. Stealing is a
widespread, common vice, but people pay so little attention to it that
the matter is entirely out of hand. If all who are thieves, though they
are unwilling to admit it, were hanged on the gallows, the world would
soon be empty, and there would be a shortage of both hangmen and
gallows. As I have just said, a person steals not only when he robs a
man's strongbox or his pocket, but also when he takes advantage of
his neighbor at the market, in a grocery shop, butcher stall, wine- and
beer-cellar, work-shop, and, in short, wherever business is transacted
and money is exchanged for goods or labor.

Let us make it a little clearer for the common people so that   225
we may see how honest we are. Suppose, for example, that a man-
servant or maid-servant is unfaithful in his or her domestic duty and
does damage or permits damage to happen when it could have been
avoided. Or suppose that through laziness, carelessness, or malice a
servant wastes and neglects things to the vexation and annoyance of
his master or mistress. When this is done deliberately—for I am not
speaking of what happens inadvertently and unintentionally—a servant
can cheat his employer out of thirty or forty gulden or more a year.
If a thief had taken such sums he would be strangled with a noose,
but the servant may even become defiant and insolent and dare anyone
to call him a thief!

The same must be said of artisans, workmen, and day-laborers   226
who act high-handedly and never know enough ways to overcharge
people and yet are careless and unreliable in their work. All these are
far worse than sneak-thieves, against whom we can guard with lock
and bolt, or if we catch them we can deal with them so that they will
not repeat the offense. But against the others no one can guard. No
one even dares to give them a hard look or accuse them of theft. One
would ten times rather lose the money from one's purse. For these
are my neighbors, my good friends, my own servants, from whom I
expect good; but they are the first to defraud me.

[8] Cf. Eph. 5:22, 25; Col. 3:18f.

Furthermore, at the market and in everyday business the same   227
fraud prevails in full force. One person openly cheats another with
defective merchandise, false measures, dishonest weights, and bad
coins, and takes advantage of him by underhanded tricks and sharp
practices and crafty dealing. Or again, one swindles another in a
trade and deliberately fleeces, skins, and torments him. Who can even
describe or imagine it all? In short, thievery is the most common   228
craft and the largest guild on earth. If we look at mankind in all its
conditions, it is nothing but a vast, wide stable full of great thieves.

These men are called gentleman swindlers[9] or big operators.   229
Far from being picklocks and sneak-thieves who loot a cash box, they
sit in office chairs and are called great lords and honorable, good
citizens, and yet with a great show of legality they rob and steal.

Yes, we might well keep quiet here about various petty   230
thieves in order to launch an attack against the great, powerful arch-
thieves who consort with lords and princes and daily plunder not only
a city or two, but all Germany. Indeed, what would become of the
head and chief protector of all thieves, the Holy See at Rome, and
all its retinue, which has plundered and stolen the treasures of the
whole world and holds them to this day?

This, in short, is the way of the world. Those who can steal   231
and rob openly are safe and free, unmolested by anyone, even claiming
honor from men. Meanwhile the little sneak-thieves who have
committed one offense must bear disgrace and punishment so as to
make the others look respectable and honorable. But the latter
should be told that in the eyes of God they are the greatest thieves,
and that he will punish them as they deserve.

This commandment is very far-reaching, as we have shown. It   232
is necessary, therefore, to emphasize and explain it to the common
people in order that they may be restrained in their wantonness and
that the wrath of God may be continually and urgently kept before
their eyes. For we must preach this not to Christians but chiefly to
knaves and scoundrels, though it might be more fitting if the judge,
the jailer, or the hangman did the preaching. Let every one   233
know, then, that it is his duty, at the risk of God's displeasure, not to
harm his neighbor, take advantage of him, or defraud him by any
faithless or underhanded business transaction. More than that, he is
under obligation faithfully to protect his neighbor's property and
further his interests, especially when he takes remuneration for such
services.

[9] Luther's word is *Stuhlräuber,* a contemporary expression for "usurers."
He takes the term to refer to men whom we might call "swivel-chair
operators." Luther's etymology, however, is wrong; *Stuhlräuber* is derived
not from *Stuhl,* meaning chair, but from the Low German *Stôl,* meaning
capital let out for interest or "rent."

A person who willfully disregards this commandment may 234
indeed get by and escape the hangman, but he will not escape God's
wrath and punishment. Though he pursues his defiant and arrogant
course for a long time, still he will remain a tramp and a beggar and
will suffer all kinds of troubles and misfortunes. Now, you 235
servants ought to take care of your master's or mistress's property,
which enables you to stuff your craw and your belly. But you go your
own way, take your wages like a thief, and even expect to be revered
like noblemen. Many of you are even insolent toward masters and
mistresses and unwilling to do them the favor and service of protecting
them from loss. But see what you gain. When you come into 236
property yourself and have a house of your own—which God will
let you acquire to your undoing—there will come a day of reckoning
and retribution: for every penny you have taken and for every penny's
damage you have done you will have to pay back thirty-fold.

So will it be with artisans and day-laborers, from whom we are 237
obliged to suffer such intolerable insolence. They act as if they were
lords over others' possessions and entitled to whatever they demand.
Just let them keep on boldly fleecing people as long as they can. 238
God will not forget his commandment. He will pay them what they
deserve. He will hang them not on a green gallows but on a dry one.[1]
They will neither prosper nor gain anything their whole life long.
Of course, if our government were well regulated, such insolence 239
might soon be checked. The ancient Romans, for example, promptly
took such offenders by the scruff of the neck so that others took
warning.

The same fate will overtake those who turn the free public 240
market into a carrion-pit and a robbers' den. Daily the poor are
defrauded. New burdens and high prices are imposed. Everyone
misuses the market in his own willful, conceited, arrogant way, as if it
were his right and privilege to sell his goods as dearly as he pleases
without a word of criticism. We shall stand by and let such 241
persons fleece, grab, and hoard. But we shall trust God, who 242
takes matters into his own hands. After they have scrimped and scraped
for a long time, he will pronounce this kind of blessing over them:
"Your grain will spoil in the garner and your beer in the cellar. Your
cattle will die in the stall. Yes, where you have cheated and defrauded
anyone out of a gulden, your entire hoard will be consumed by rust
so that you will never enjoy it."

Indeed, we have the evidence before our very eyes every day 243
that no stolen or ill-gotten possession thrives. How many people scrape
and scratch day and night and yet grow not a penny richer! Though

---

[1] Death on the gallows was considered a more ignominious punishment
than death on a green tree ("green gallows").

they gather a great hoard, they must suffer so many troubles and misfortunes that they can never enjoy it or pass it on to their children. But because we ignore this and act as if it were none of our 244 business, God must punish us and teach us morals in a different way. He lays on us one affliction after another, or he quarters a troop of soldiers upon us; in one hour they clean out our chests and purse down to the last penny, and then by way of thanks they burn and ravage house and home and outrage and kill wife and children.

In short, however much you steal, depend on it that just as 245 much will be stolen from you. Anyone who robs and takes things by violence and dishonesty must put up with another who plays the same game. For God is a master of this art; since everyone robs and steals from the other, he punishes one thief by means of another. Otherwise, where would we find enough gallows and ropes?

Whoever is willing to learn a lesson, let him know that this 246 is God's commandment and must not be treated as a joke. We shall put up with those of you who despise, defraud, steal, and rob us. We shall endure your arrogance and show forgiveness and mercy, as the Lord's Prayer teaches. The upright, meanwhile, will not want, and you will hurt yourself more than others. But beware how you deal with the poor, of whom there are many now. If, when you meet a 247 poor man who must live from hand to mouth, you act as if everyone must live by your favor, you skin and scrape him right down to the bone, and you arrogantly turn him away whom you ought to give aid, he will go away wretched and dejected, and because he can complain to no one else, he will cry to heaven. Beware of this, I repeat, as of the devil himself. Such a man's sighs and cries will be no joking matter. They will have an effect too heavy for you and all the world to bear, for they will reach God, who watches over poor, sorrowful hearts, and he will not leave them unavenged. But if you despise and defy this, see whom you have brought upon yourself. If you succeed and prosper, before all the world you may call God and me liars.

We have now given sufficient warning and exhortation. He 248 who will not heed or believe this may go his own way until he learns it by experience. But it needs to be impressed upon the young people so that they may be on their guard and not follow the old, wayward crowd, but may keep their eyes fixed upon God's commandment, lest his wrath and punishment come upon them too. Our responsibility 249 is only to instruct and reprove by means of God's Word. To restrain open lawlessness is the responsibility of princes and magistrates. They should be alert and resolute enough to establish and maintain order in all areas of trade and commerce in order that the poor may not be burdened and oppressed and in order that they may not themselves be charged with other men's sins.

Enough has been said concerning the nature of stealing. It is 250

not to be confined to narrow limits but must extend to all our
relations with our neighbors. To sum up, as we have done in the
previous commandments: On one hand, we are forbidden to do our
neighbor any injury or wrong in any way imaginable, whether by
damaging, withholding, or interfering with his possessions and
property. We are not even to consent to or permit such a thing, but
are rather to avert and prevent it. On the other hand, we are   251
commanded to promote and further our neighbor's interests, and when
he suffers want we are to help, share, and lend to both friends and foes.

Anyone who seeks and desires good works will here find   252
ample opportunity to do things which are heartily acceptable and
pleasing to God. Moreover, he graciously lavishes upon them a
wonderful blessing: We shall be richly rewarded for all the help and
kindness we show to our neighbor, as King Solomon teaches in
Prov. 19:17, "He who is kind to the poor lends to the Lord, and he
will repay him for his deed." Here you have a rich Lord.   253
Surely he is sufficient for your needs and will let you lack or want
for nothing. Thus with a happy conscience you can enjoy a hundred
times more than you could scrape together by perfidy and injustice.
Whoever does not desire this blessing will find wrath and misfortune
enough.

THE EIGHTH COMMANDMENT

"You shall not bear false witness against your neighbor."   254

Besides our own body, our wife or husband, and our temporal   255
property, we have one more treasure which is indispensable to us,
namely, our honor and good name, for it is intolerable to live among
men in public disgrace and contempt. Therefore God will not   256
have our neighbor deprived of his reputation, honor, and character
any more than of his money and possessions; he would have every man
maintain his self-respect before his wife, children, servants, and
neighbors. In its first and simplest meaning, as the words stand   257
("You shall not bear false witness"), this commandment pertains to
public courts of justice, where a poor, innocent man is accused and
maligned by false witnesses and consequently punished in his body,
property, or honor.

This problem appears to concern us only a little at present, but   258
among the Jews it was extremely common. That nation had an
excellent, orderly government, and even now, where there is such a
government, instances of this sin still occur. The reason is this:
Where judges, mayors, princes, or others in authority sit in judgment,
we always find that, true to the usual course of the world, men are
loath to offend anyone. Instead, they speak dishonestly with an eye
to gaining favor, money, prospects, or friendship. Consequently, a
poor man is inevitably oppressed, loses his case, and suffers punish-

ment. It is the universal misfortune of the world that men of integrity seldom preside in courts of justice.

A judge ought, above all, to be a man of integrity, and not   259 only upright but also a wise, sagacious, brave, and fearless man. Likewise, a witness should be fearless; more than that, he should be an upright man. He who is to administer justice equitably in all cases will often offend good friends, relatives, neighbors, and the rich and powerful who are in a position to help or harm him. He must therefore be quite blind, shutting his eyes and ears to everything but the evidence presented, and make his decision accordingly.

The first application of this commandment, then, is that   260 everyone should help his neighbor maintain his rights. He must not allow these rights to be thwarted or distorted but should promote and resolutely guard them, whether he be judge or witness, let the consequences be what they may. Here we have a goal set for our   261 jurists: perfect justice and equity in every case. They should let right remain right, not perverting or concealing or suppressing anything on account of anyone's money, property, honor, or power. This is one aspect of the commandment, and its plainest meaning, applying to all that takes place in court.

Next, it extends much further when it is applied to spiritual   262 jurisdiction or administration. Here, too, everyone bears false witness against his neighbor. Wherever there are godly preachers and Christians, they must endure having the world call them heretics, apostates, even seditious and accursed scoundrels. Moreover, the Word of God must undergo the most shameful and spiteful persecution and blasphemy; it is contradicted, perverted, misused, and misinterpreted. But let this pass; it is the blind world's nature to condemn and persecute the truth and the children of God and yet consider this no sin.

The third aspect of this commandment concerns us all. It   263 forbids all sins of the tongue by which we may injure or offend our neighbor. False witness is clearly a work of the tongue. Whatever is done with the tongue against a neighbor, then, is forbidden by God. This applies to false preachers with their corrupt teaching and blasphemy, to false judges and witnesses with their corrupt behavior in court and their lying and malicious talk outside of court. It   264 applies particularly to the detestable, shameful vice of back-biting or slander by which the devil rides us. Of this much could be said. It is a common vice of human nature that everyone would rather hear evil than good about his neighbor. Evil though we are, we cannot tolerate having evil spoken of us; we want the golden compliments of the whole world. Yet we cannot bear to hear the best spoken of others.

To avoid this vice, therefore, we should note that nobody has   265 the right to judge and reprove his neighbor publicly, even when he has seen a sin committed, unless he has been authorized to judge and reprove. There is a great difference between judging sin and 266 having knowledge of sin. Knowledge of sin does not entail the right to judge it. I may see and hear that my neighbor sins, but to make him the talk of the town is not my business. If I interfere and pass sentence on him, I fall into a greater sin than his. When you become aware of a sin, simply make your ears a tomb and bury it until you are appointed a judge and authorized to administer punishment by virtue of your office.

Those are called backbiters who are not content just to know 267 but rush ahead and judge. Learning a bit of gossip about someone else, they spread it into every corner, relishing and delighting in it like pigs that roll in the mud and root around in it with their snouts. This 268 is nothing else than usurping the judgment and office of God, pronouncing the severest kind of verdict and sentence, or the harshest verdict a judge can pronounce is to declare somebody a thief, a murderer, a traitor, etc. Whoever therefore ventures to accuse his neighbor of such guilt assumes as much authority as the emperor and all magistrates. For though you do not wield the sword, you use your venomous tongue to the disgrace and harm of your neighbor.

Therefore God forbids you to speak evil about another even 269 though, to your certain knowledge, he is guilty. All the more urgent is the prohibition if you are not sure but have it only from hearsay. But you say: "Why shouldn't I speak if it is the truth?" I reply: 270 "Why don't you bring it before the regular judge?" "Oh, I cannot prove it publicly; I might be called a liar and sent away in disgrace." Ah, now do you smell the roast? If you do not trust yourself to make your charges before the proper authorities, then hold your tongue. Keep your knowledge to yourself and do not give it out to others. For when you repeat a story that you cannot prove, even if it is true, you appear as a liar. Besides, you act like a knave, for no man should be deprived of his honor and good name unless these have first been taken away from him publicly.

Every report, then, that cannot be adequately proved is false 271 witness. No one should publicly assert as truth what is not 272 publicly substantiated. In short, what is secret should be allowed to remain secret, or at any rate be reproved in secret, as we shall hear. Therefore, if you encounter somebody with a worthless tongue 273 who gossips and slanders someone, rebuke him straight to his face and make him blush for shame. Then you will silence many a one who otherwise would bring some poor man into disgrace, from which he could scarcely clear himself. For honor and good name are easily taken away, but not easily restored.

So you see that we are absolutely forbidden to speak evil of 274 our neighbor. Exception is made, however, of civil magistrates, preachers, and parents, for we must interpret this commandment in such a way that evil shall not go unpunished. We have seen that the Fifth Commandment forbids us to injure anyone physically, and yet an exception is made of the hangman. By virtue of his office he does not do his neighbor good but only harm and evil, yet he does not sin against God's commandment because God of his own accord instituted that office, and as he warns in the Fifth Commandment, he has reserved to himself the right of punishment. Likewise, although no one has in his own person the right to judge and condemn anyone, yet if they whose duty it is fail to do so, they sin as much as those who take the law into their own hands without such a commission. Necessity requires one to report evil, to prefer charges, to attest, 275 examine, and witness. It is no different from the situation of the physician who, to cure a patient, is sometimes compelled to examine and handle his private parts. Just so, magistrates, parents, even brothers and sisters and other good friends are under mutual obligation to reprove evil where it is necessary and beneficial.

But the right way to deal with this matter would be to observe 276 the order laid down by the Gospel, Matthew 19,[2] where Christ says, "If your brother sins against you, go and tell him his fault, between you and him alone." Here you have a fine, precious precept for governing the tongue which ought to be carefully noted if we are to avoid this detestable abuse. Let this be your rule, then, that you should not be quick to spread slander and gossip about your neighbor but admonish him privately so that he may amend. Likewise, if someone should whisper to you what this or that person has done, teach him, if he saw the wrongdoing, to go and reprove the man personally, otherwise to hold his tongue.

This lesson you can learn from the daily management of the 277 household. When the master of the house sees a servant failing to do his duty, he takes him to task personally. If he were so foolish as to leave the servant at home while he went out on the streets to complain to his neighbors, he would no doubt be told: "You fool! That is none of our business. Why don't you tell him yourself?" And that would be the brotherly thing to say, for the evil would 278 be corrected and the neighbor's honor maintained. As Christ himself says in the same passage, "If he listens to you, you have gained your brother." Then you have done a great and excellent work. Do you think it is an insignificant thing to gain a brother? Let all monks and holy orders step forth, with all their works heaped up together, and see if they can make the boast that they have gained one brother!

Christ teaches further: "If he does not listen, take one or two 279 others along with you, that every word may be confirmed by the

---

[2] Matt. 18:15. The reference was corrected in later editions.

evidence of two or three witnesses." [3] So the individual is to be dealt with personally and not gossiped about behind his back. If this 280 does not help, then bring the matter before the public, either before the civil or the ecclesiastical court. Then you do not stand alone. You have witnesses with you through whom you can convict the guilty one and on whose testimony the judge can base his decision and sentence. This is the right procedure for restraining and reforming a wicked person. But if you gossip about someone in every corner 281 and root around in the filth, nobody will be reformed. Moreover, when you are called upon to witness, you will probably deny having said anything. It would serve such gossips right to have their 282 sport spoiled, as a warning to others. If you were acting for 283 your neighbor's improvement or from love of the truth, you would not sneak about in secret, shunning the light of day.

All this refers to secret sins. But where the sin is so public 284 that the judge and the whole world are aware of it, you can without sin shun and avoid the person as one who has brought disgrace upon himself, and you may testify publicly concerning him. For when an affair is manifest to everybody there can be no question of slander or injustice or false witness. For example, we now censure the pope and his teaching, which is publicly set forth in books and shouted throughout the world. Where the sin is public, the punishment ought to be public so that everyone may know how to guard against it.

Now we have the sum and substance of this commandment: 285 No one shall harm his neighbor, whether friend or foe, with his tongue. No one shall speak evil of him, whether truly or falsely, unless it is done with proper authority or for his improvement. A person should use his tongue to speak only good of everyone, to cover his neighbor's sins and infirmities, to overlook them, and to cloak and veil them with his own honor. Our chief reason for doing so 286 should be the one which Christ indicates in the Gospel, and in which he means to embrace all the commandments concerning our neighbor, "Whatever you wish that men would do to you, do so to them." [4]

Even nature teaches the same thing in our own bodies, as 287 St. Paul says in I Cor. 12:22, 23, "The parts of the body which seem to be weaker are indispensable, and those parts of the body which we think less honorable we invest with the greater honor; and our unpresentable parts are treated with greater modesty." No one covers his face, eyes, nose, and mouth; we do not need to, for they are our most honorable members. But the weakest members, of which we are ashamed, we carefully conceal. Our hands and eyes, even the whole body, must help to cover and veil them. Thus in our relations 288

[3] Matt. 18:16.
[4] Matt. 7:12.

with one another, we should veil whatever blemishes and infirmities we find in our neighbor, doing our utmost to serve and help him to promote his honor. On the other hand, we should prevent everything that tends to his disgrace. It is a particularly fine, noble virtue   289 always to put the best construction upon all we may hear about our neighbor, as long as it is not a notorious evil, and to defend him against the poisonous tongues of those who are busy wherever they can pry out and pounce on something to criticize in their neighbor, misconstruing and twisting things in the worst way. This is what happens now especially to the precious Word of God and its preachers.

This commandment, then, embraces a great multitude of good   290 works which please God most highly and bring abundant blessings, if only the blind world and the false saints would recognize them. There is nothing about a man or in a man that can do greater   291 good or greater harm, in spiritual or in temporal matters, than this smallest and weakest of his members, the tongue.[5]

THE NINTH AND TENTH COMMANDMENTS

"You shall not covet your neighbor's house."   292
"You shall not covet his wife, man-servant, maid-servant, cattle, or anything that is his."

These two commandments, taken literally, were given exclu-   293 sively to the Jews; nevertheless, in part they also apply to us. The Jews did not interpret them as referring to unchastity or theft, since these vices were sufficiently forbidden in commandments above. They thought they were keeping the commandments when they obeyed the injunctions and prohibitions contained in them. God therefore added these two commandments to teach them that it is sinful and forbidden to covet our neighbor's wife or property, or to have any designs upon them. Especially were these commandments needed   294 because under the Jewish government man-servants and maid-servants were not free, as now, to serve for wages according to their own choice; with their body and all they had they were their master's property, the same as his cattle and other possessions. Moreover,   295 every man had power to dismiss his wife publicly by giving her a bill of divorce[6] and to take another wife. So there was a danger among them that if anyone took a fancy to another's wife, he might on any flimsy excuse dismiss his own wife and estrange the other's from him so that he might legally take her. They considered this no more a sin or disgrace than it is now for a master to dismiss his servants or entice his neighbor's from him.

Therefore, I say, they interpreted these commandments   296

---

[5] Cf. James 3:5.
[6] Cf. Deut. 24:1.

correctly (though they also have a broader and higher application) to forbid anyone, even with a specious pretext, to covet or scheme to despoil his neighbor of what belongs to him, such as his wife, servants, house, fields, meadows, or cattle. Above, the seventh commandment prohibits seizing or withholding another's possessions to which you have no right. But here it is also forbidden to entice anything away from your neighbor, even though in the eyes of the world you could do it honorably, without accusation or blame for fraudulent dealing.

Such is nature that we all begrudge another's having as much   297 as we have. Everyone acquires all he can and lets others look out for themselves. Yet we all pretend to be upright. We know how to   298 put up a fine front to conceal our rascality. We think up artful dodges and sly tricks (better and better ones are being devised daily) under the guise of justice. We brazenly dare to boast of it, and insist that it should be called not rascality but shrewdness and business acumen. In this we are abetted by jurists and lawyers who twist and stretch   299 the law to suit their purpose, straining words and using them for pretexts, without regard for equity or for our neighbor's plight. In short, whoever is sharpest and shrewdest in such affairs gets most advantage out of the law, for as the saying has it, "The law favors the vigilant."

This last commandment, then, is addressed not to those whom   300 the world considers wicked rogues, but precisely to the most upright— to people who wish to be commended as honest and virtuous because they have not offended against the preceding commandments. To this class the Jews especially claimed to belong, as many great nobles, lords, and princes do now. For the common masses belong much farther down in the scale, where the Seventh Commandment applies, since they are not much concerned about questions of honor and right when it comes to acquiring possessions.

This situation occurs most frequently in lawsuits in which   301 someone sets out to gain and squeeze something out of his neighbor. For example, when people wrangle and wrestle over a large inheritance, real estate, etc., they resort to whatever arguments have the least semblance of right, so varnishing and garnishing them that the law supports them, and they gain such secure title to the property as to put it beyond complaint or dispute. Similarly, if anyone covets   302 a castle, city, county, or other great estate, he practices bribery, through friendly connections and by any other means at his disposal, until the property is taken away from the owner and legally awarded to him with letters patent and the seal of the prince attesting that it was acquired lawfully.

The same thing happens in ordinary business affairs, where one   303 cunningly slips something out of another's hand so that the victim is helpless to prevent it. Or, seeing an opportunity for profit—let us say, when a man because of adversity or debt cannot hold on to his property, nor yet sell it without loss—he hurries and worries him until he acquires a half or more of it; and yet this must not be considered as illegally acquired, but rather as honestly purchased. Hence the sayings, "First come, first served," and "Every man must look out for himself while others shift for themselves." Who is ingenious 304 enough to imagine how much he can acquire by such specious pretexts? The world does not consider this wrong, and it does not see that the neighbor is being taken advantage of and forced to sacrifice what he cannot spare without injury. Yet no one wishes this to happen to himself. From this it is clear that all these pretexts and shams are false.

This was also the case in ancient times with respect to wives. 305 They knew tricks like this: If a man took a fancy to another woman, he managed, either personally or through others and by any of a number of ways, to make her husband displeased with her, or she became so disobedient and hard to live with that her husband was obliged to dismiss her and leave her to the other man. That sort of thing undoubtedly was quite prevalent in the time of the law, for we read even in the Gospel[7] that King Herod took his brother's wife while the latter was still living, and yet posed as an honorable, upright man, as St. Mark testifies. Such examples, I trust, will not be 306 found among us, except that someone may by trickery entice a rich bride away from another, for in the New Testament[8] married people are forbidden to be divorced. But it is not uncommon among us for a person to lure away another's man-servant or maid-servant or otherwise estrange them with fair words.

However these things may be, you must learn that God does 307 not wish you to deprive your neighbor of anything that is his, letting him suffer loss while you gratify your greed, even though in the eyes of the world you might honorably retain the property. To do so is dark and underhanded wickedness, and, as we say, it is all done "under the hat"[9] so as to escape detection. Although you may act as if you have wronged no one, you have trespassed on your neighbor's rights. It may not be called stealing or fraud, yet it is coveting—that is, having designs upon your neighbor's property, luring it away from him against his will, and begrudging what God gave him. The 308 judge and the public may have to leave you in possession of it, but God will not, for he sees your wicked heart and the deceitfulness of the world. If you give the world an inch, it will take a yard, and at length open injustice and violence follow.

Let these commandments therefore retain their general appli- 309

[7] Matt. 14:3f.; Mark 6:17ff.
[8] Matt. 5:31f., 19:3-9; Mark 10:2-12; Luke 16:18; I Cor. 7:10f.
[9] An expression derived from sorcery.

cation. We are commanded not to desire harm to our neighbor, nor become accessory to it, nor give occasion for it; we are willingly to leave him what is his, and promote and protect whatever may be profitable and serviceable to him, as we wish that he would do to us. Thus these commandments are directed especially against envy 310 and miserable covetousness, God's purpose being to destroy all the roots and causes of our injuries to our neighbors. Therefore he sets it forth in plain words: "You shall not covet," etc. Above all, he wants our hearts to be pure, even though as long as we live here we cannot reach that ideal. So this commandment remains, like all the rest, one that constantly accuses us and shows just how upright we really are in God's sight.

Conclusion of the Ten Commandments[1]

Here, then, we have the Ten Commandments, a summary of 311 divine teaching on what we are to do to make our whole life pleasing to God. They are the true fountain from which all good works must spring, the true channel through which all good works must flow. Apart from these Ten Commandments no deed, no conduct can be good or pleasing to God, no matter how great or precious it may be in the eyes of the world.

Let us see, now, how our great saints can boast of their 312 spiritual orders and the great, difficult works which they have fashioned while they neglect these commandments as if they were too insignificant or had been fulfilled long ago.

It seems to me that we shall have our hands full to keep these 313 commandments, practicing gentleness, patience, love toward enemies, chastity, kindness, etc., and all that these virtues involve. But such works are not important or impressive in the eyes of the world. They are not unusual and pompous, restricted to special times, places, rites, and ceremonies, but are common, everyday domestic duties of one neighbor toward another, with no show about them. On the other 314 hand, those other works captivate all eyes and ears. Aided by great pomp, splendor, and magnificent buildings, they are so adorned that everything gleams and glitters. There is burning of incense, singing and ringing of bells, lighting of tapers and candles until nothing else can be seen or heard. For when a priest stands in a gold-embroidered chasuble[2] or a layman remains on his knees a whole day in church, this is considered a precious work that cannot be sufficiently extolled. But when a poor girl tends a little child, or faithfully does what she is told, that is regarded as nothing. Otherwise, why should monks and nuns go into cloisters?

---

[1] This title was inserted later.

[2] An elaborate vestment for the officiant at Mass. Cf. Smalcald Articles, Preface, 13.

Just think, is it not a devilish presumption on the part of those   315
desperate saints to dare to find a higher and better way of life than
the Ten Commandments teach? They pretend, as we have said, that
this is a simple life for the ordinary man, whereas theirs is for the
saints and the perfect. They fail to see, these miserable, blind   316
people, that no man can achieve so much as to keep one of the Ten
Commandments as it ought to be kept. Both the Creed and the Lord's
Prayer must help us, as we shall hear. Through them we must seek
and pray for help and receive it continually. Therefore all their
boasting amounts to as much as if I boasted, "Of course, I haven't a
single groschen to pay, but I promise to pay ten gulden." [3]

All this I say and repeat in order that men may get rid of the   317
pernicious abuse which has become so deeply rooted and still clings to
every man, and that all classes of men on earth may accustom themselves to look only to these precepts and heed them. It will be a long
time before men produce a doctrine or social order equal to that
of the Ten Commandments, for they are beyond human power to
fulfill. Anyone who does fulfill them is a heavenly, angelic man, far
above all holiness on earth. Just concentrate upon them and   318
test yourself thoroughly, do your very best, and you will surely find
so much to do that you will neither seek nor pay attention to any
other works or other kind of holiness.

Let this suffice concerning the first part,[4] both for instruction   319
and for admonition. In conclusion, however, we must repeat the text
which we have already treated above in connection with the First
Commandment[5] in order to show how much effort God requires us to
devote to learning how to teach and practice the Ten Commandments.

"I the Lord, your God, am a jealous God, visiting the iniquity   320
of the fathers upon the children to the third and fourth generation of
them that hate me; but to those who love and keep my commandments,
I show mercy unto a thousand generations."

Although primarily attached to the First Commandment, as we   321
heard above, this appendix was intended to apply to all the commandments, and all of them as a whole ought to be referred and directed
to it. For this reason I said that we should keep it before the young
and insist that they learn and remember it so that we may see why we
are constrained and compelled to keep these Ten Commandments.
This appendix ought to be regarded as attached to each individual
commandment, penetrating and pervading them all.

Now, as we said before, these words contain both a wrathful   322
threat and a friendly promise, not only to terrify and warn us but also

[3] There were 21 groschen, small gold or silver coins (English: groat), to a
gulden.
[4] I.e., the first part of the Catechism.
[5] Section 30, above.

to attract and allure us. These words, therefore, ought to be received and esteemed as a serious matter to God because he himself here declares how important the commandments are to him and how strictly he will watch over them, fearfully and terribly punishing all who despise and transgress his commandments; and again, how richly he will reward, bless, and bestow all good things on those who prize them and gladly act and live in accordance with them. Thus he 323 demands that all our actions proceed from a heart that fears and regards God alone and, because of this fear, avoids all that is contrary to his will, lest he be moved to wrath; and, conversely, trusts him alone and for his sake does all that he asks of us, because he shows himself a kind father and offers us every grace and blessing.

This is exactly the meaning and right interpretation of the 324 first and chief commandment, from which all the others proceed. This word, "You shall have no other gods," means simply, "You shall fear, love, and trust me as your one true God." Wherever a man's heart has such an attitude toward God, he has fulfilled this commandment and all the others. On the other hand, whoever fears and loves anything else in heaven and on earth will keep neither this nor any other. Thus the entire Scriptures have proclaimed and presented 325 this commandment everywhere, emphasizing these two things, fear of God and trust in God. The prophet David particularly teaches it throughout the Psalter, as when he says, "The Lord takes pleasure in those who fear him, in those who hope in his mercy" (Ps. 147:11). He seems to explain the whole commandment in one verse, as if to say, "The Lord takes pleasure in those who have no other gods."

Thus the First Commandment is to illuminate and impart its 326 splendor to all the others. In order that this may be constantly repeated and never forgotten, therefore, you must let these concluding words run through all the commandments, like the clasp or the hoop of a wreath that binds the end to the beginning and holds everything together. For example, in the Second Commandment we are told to fear God and not take his name in vain by cursing, lying, deceiving, and other kinds of corruption and wickedness, but to use his name properly by calling upon him in prayer, praise, and thanksgiving, which spring from that love and trust which the First Commandment requires. Similarly, this fear, love, and trust should impel us not to despise his Word, but learn it, hear it gladly, keep it holy, and honor it.

So, through the following commandments which concern our 327 neighbor, everything proceeds from the force of the First Commandment: We are to honor father and mother, masters, and all in authority, being submissive and obedient to them not on their own account but for God's sake. For you dare not respect or fear father or mother wrongly, doing or omitting to do things simply in order to please them. Rather, ask what God wants of you and what he will quite surely demand of you. If you omit that, you have an angry judge; otherwise, you have a gracious father.

Again, you are to do your neighbor no harm, injury, or 328 violence, nor in any way molest him, either in his person, his wife, his property, his honor or rights, as these things are commanded in that order, even though you have the opportunity and occasion to do so and no man may reprove you. On the contrary, you should do good to all men, help them and promote their interests, however and whenever you can, purely out of love to God and in order to please him, in the confidence that he will abundantly reward you for all you do. Thus you see how the First Commandment is the chief 329 source and fountainhead from which all the others proceed; again, to it they all return and upon it they depend, so that end and beginning are all linked and bound together.

It is useful and necessary always to teach, admonish, and 330 remind young people of all this so that they may be brought up, not only with blows and compulsion, like cattle, but in the fear and reverence of God. These are not trifles of men but the commandments of the most high God, who watches over them with great earnestness, who vents his wrath upon those who despise them, and, on the contrary, abundantly rewards those who keep them. Where men consider this and take it to heart, there will arise a spontaneous impulse and desire gladly to do God's will. Therefore it is not without 331 reason that the Old Testament commands men to write the Ten Commandments on every wall and corner, and even on their garments.[6] Not that we are to have them there merely for a display, as the Jews did,[7] but we are to keep them incessantly before our eyes and constantly in our memory, and practice them in all our works and ways. Everyone is to make them his daily habit in all 332 circumstances, in all his affairs and dealings, as if they were written everywhere he looks, and even wherever he goes or wherever he stands. Thus, both for himself at home, and abroad among his neighbors, he will find occasion enough to practice the Ten Commandments, and no one need search far for them.

From all this it is obvious once again how highly these Ten 333 Commandments are to be exalted and extolled above all orders, commands, and works which are taught and practiced apart from them. Here we can fling out the challenge: Let all wise men and saints step forward and produce, if they can, any work like that which God in these commandments so earnestly requires and enjoins under threat of his greatest wrath and punishment, while at the same time he adds such glorious promises that he will shower us with all good things and

[6] Deut. 6:8f., 11:20.
[7] Cf. Matt. 23:5.

blessings. Therefore we should prize and value them above all other teachings as the greatest treasure God has given us.

SECOND PART: THE CREED

Thus far we have heard the first part of Christian doctrine. In it 1 we have seen all that God wishes us to do or not to do. The Creed properly follows, setting forth all that we must expect and receive from God; in brief, it teaches us to know him perfectly. It is given 2 in order to help us do what the Ten Commandments require of us. For, as we said above, they are set on so high a plane that all human ability is far too feeble and weak to keep them. Therefore it is as necessary to learn this part as it is the other so that we may know where and how to obtain strength for this task. If we could by our 3 own strength keep the Ten Commandments as they ought to be kept, we would need neither the Creed nor the Lord's Prayer. But before 4 we explain the advantage and necessity of the Creed, it is sufficient, as a first step, for very simple persons to learn to understand the Creed itself.

In the first place, the Creed used to be divided into twelve 5 articles.[8] Of course, if all the thoughts contained in the Scriptures and belonging to the Creed were gathered together, there would be many more articles, nor could they all be clearly expressed in so few words. But to make it most clear and simple for teaching to children, we 6 shall briefly sum up the entire Creed in three articles,[9] according to the three persons of the Godhead, to whom all that we believe is related. The first article, of God the Father, explains creation; the second, of the Son, redemption; the third, of the Holy Spirit, sanctification. Hence the Creed may be briefly comprised in these few words: "I 7 believe in God the Father, who created me; I believe in God the Son, who redeemed me; I believe in the Holy Spirit, who sanctifies me." One God and one faith, but three persons, and therefore three articles or confessions. Let us briefly comment on these words.   8

THE FIRST ARTICLE

"I believe in God, the Father almighty, maker of heaven and 9 *earth."*

These words give us a brief description of God the Father, his 10 nature, his will, and his work. Since the Ten Commandments have explained that we are to have no more than one God, it may be asked:

[8] Tradition, dating to about A.D. 400, held that each of the twelve apostles contributed one article to the Creed.

[9] Luther proposed the three-fold division in "A Brief Form of the Creed" (1520), *WA*, 7:214.

"What kind of being is God? What does he do? How can we praise or portray or describe him in such a way as to make him known?" This is taught here and in the following articles. Thus the Creed is nothing else than a response and confession of Christians based on the First Commandment. If you were to ask a young child, "My boy, 11 what kind of God have you? What do you know about him?" he could say, "First, my God is the Father, who made heaven and earth. Apart from him alone I have no other God, for there is no one else who could create heaven and earth."

For the somewhat more advanced and the educated, however, 12 all three articles can be treated more fully and divided into as many parts as there are words. But for young pupils it is enough to indicate the most necessary points, namely, as we have said, that this article deals with creation. We should emphasize the words, "maker of heaven and earth." What is meant by these words, "I believe in 13 God, the Father almighty, maker," etc.? Answer: I hold and believe that I am a creature of God; that is, that he has given and constantly sustains my body, soul, and life, my members great and small, all the faculties of my mind, my reason and understanding, and so forth; my food and drink, clothing, means of support, wife and child, servants, house and home, etc. Besides, he makes all creation help 14 provide the comforts and necessities of life—sun, moon, and stars in the heavens, day and night, air, fire, water, the earth and all that it brings forth, birds and fish, beasts, grain and all kinds of produce. Moreover, he gives all physical and temporal blessings—good 15 government, peace, security. Thus we learn from this article that 16 none of us has his life of himself, or anything else that has been mentioned here or can be mentioned, nor can he by himself preserve any of them, however small and unimportant. All this is comprehended in the word "Creator."

Moreover, we confess that God the Father not only has given 17 us all that we have and see before our eyes, but also daily guards and defends us against every evil and misfortune, warding off all sorts of danger and disaster. All this he does out of pure love and goodness, without our merit, as a kind father who cares for us so that no evil may befall us. But further discussion of this subject belongs in 18 the other two parts of this article, where we say, "Father almighty."

Hence, since everything we possess, and everything in heaven 19 and on earth besides, is daily given and sustained by God, it inevitably follows that we are in duty bound to love, praise, and thank him without ceasing, and, in short, to devote all these things to his service, as he has required and enjoined in the Ten Commandments.

Much could be said if we were to describe in detail how few 20 people believe this article. We all pass over it, hear it, and recite it, but we neither see nor consider what the words enjoin on us. For 21 if we believed it with our whole heart, we would also act accordingly, and not swagger about and brag and boast as if we had life, riches, power, honor, and such things of ourselves, as if we ourselves were to be feared and served. This is the way the wretched, perverse world acts, drowned in its blindness, misusing all the blessings and gifts of God solely for its own pride and greed, pleasure and enjoyment, and never once turning to God to thank him or acknowledge him as Lord and Creator.

Therefore, this article would humble and terrify us all if we 22 believed it. For we sin daily with eyes and ears, hands, body and soul, money and property, and with all that we have. This is especially true of those who even fight against the Word of God. Yet Christians have this advantage, that they acknowledge themselves in duty bound to serve and obey him for all these things.

For this reason we ought daily to study this article and impress 23 it upon our minds. Everything we see, and every blessing that comes our way, should remind us of it. When we escape distress or danger, we should recognize that this is God's doing. He gives us all these things so that we may sense and see in them his fatherly heart and his boundless love toward us. Thus our hearts will be warmed and kindled with gratitude to God and a desire to use all these blessings to his glory and praise.

Such, very briefly, is the meaning of this article. It is all that 24 ordinary people need to learn at first, both about what we have and receive from God and about what we owe him in return. This is an excellent knowledge, but an even greater treasure. For here we see how the Father has given himself to us, with all his creatures, has abundantly provided for us in this life, and, further, has showered us with inexpressible eternal treasures through his Son and the Holy Spirit, as we shall hear.

The Second Article

"And in Jesus Christ, his only Son, our Lord: who was conceived 25 *by the Holy Spirit, born of the virgin Mary, suffered under Pontius Pilate, was crucified, dead, and buried: he descended into hell, the third day he rose from the dead, he ascended into heaven, and is seated on the right hand of God, the Father almighty, whence he shall come to judge the living and the dead."*

Here we learn to know the second person of the Godhead, and 26 we see what we receive from God over and above the temporal goods mentioned above—that is, how he has completely given himself to us, withholding nothing. This article is very rich and far-reaching, but in order to treat it briefly and simply, we shall take up one phrase which contains the substance of the article; from it we shall learn how we are redeemed. We shall concentrate on these words, "in Jesus Christ, our Lord."

If you are asked, "What do you believe in the Second Article,   27 concerning Jesus Christ?" answer briefly, "I believe that Jesus Christ, true Son of God, has become my Lord." What is it to "become a Lord"? It means that he has redeemed me from sin, from the devil, from death, and from all evil. Before this I had no Lord and King but was captive under the power of the devil. I was condemned to death and entangled in sin and blindness.

When we were created by God the Father, and had received   28 from him all kinds of good things, the devil came and led us into disobedience, sin, death, and all evil. We lay under God's wrath and displeasure, doomed to eternal damnation, as we had deserved. There was no counsel, no help, no comfort for us until this only   29 and eternal Son of God, in his unfathomable goodness, had mercy on our misery and wretchedness and came from heaven to help us. Those tyrants and jailers now have been routed, and their place   30 has been taken by Jesus Christ, the Lord of life and righteousness and every good and blessing. He has snatched us, poor lost creatures, from the jaws of hell, won us, made us free, and restored us to the Father's favor and grace. He has taken us as his own, under his protection, in order that he may rule us by his righteousness, wisdom, power, life, and blessedness.

Let this be the summary of this article, that the little word   31 "Lord" simply means the same as Redeemer, that is, he who has brought us back from the devil to God, from death to life, from sin to righteousness, and now keeps us safe there. The remaining parts of this article simply serve to clarify and express how and by what means this redemption was accomplished—that is, how much it cost Christ and what he paid and risked in order to win us and bring us under his dominion. That is to say, he became man, conceived and born without sin, of the Holy Spirit and the Virgin, that he might become Lord over sin; moreover, he suffered, died, and was buried that he might make satisfaction for me and pay what I owed, not with silver and gold but with his own precious blood. All this in order to become my Lord. For he did none of these things for himself, nor had he any need of them. Afterward he rose again from the dead, swallowed up[1] and devoured death, and finally ascended into heaven and assumed dominion at the right hand of the Father. The devil and all powers, therefore, must be subject to him and lie beneath his feet until finally, at the last day, he will completely divide and separate us from the wicked world, the devil, death, sin, etc.

But the proper place to explain all these different points is not   32

---

[1] Cf. Isa. 25:8.

the brief children's sermons, but rather the longer sermons throughout the year, especially at the times appointed[2] for dealing at length with such articles as the birth, passion, resurrection, and ascension of Christ.

Indeed, the entire Gospel that we preach depends on the proper 33 understanding of this article. Upon it all our salvation and blessedness are based, and it is so rich and broad that we can never learn it fully.

THE THIRD ARTICLE

"I believe in the Holy Spirit, the holy Christian church, the 34 communion of saints, the forgiveness of sins, the resurrection of the body, and the life everlasting. Amen."

To this article, as I have said, I cannot give a better title than 35 "Sanctification." In it is expressed and portrayed the Holy Spirit and his office, which is that he makes us holy. Therefore, we must concentrate on the term "Holy Spirit," because it is so precise that we can find no substitute for it. Many other kinds of spirits are 36 mentioned in the Scriptures, such as the spirit of man,[3] heavenly spirits,[4] and the evil spirit.[5] But God's Spirit alone is called Holy Spirit, that is, he who has sanctified and still sanctifies us. As the Father is called Creator and the Son is called Redeemer, so on account of his work the Holy Spirit must be called Sanctifier, the One who makes holy. How does this sanctifying take place? Answer: Just as the 37 Son obtains dominion by purchasing us through his birth, death, and resurrection, etc., so the Holy Spirit effects our sanctification through the following: the communion of saints or Christian church, the forgiveness of sins, the resurrection of the body, and the life everlasting. In other words, he first leads us into his holy community, placing us upon the bosom of the church, where he preaches to us and brings us to Christ.

Neither you nor I could ever know anything of Christ, or believe 38 in him and take him as our Lord, unless these were first offered to us and bestowed on our hearts through the preaching of the Gospel by the Holy Spirit. The work is finished and completed, Christ has acquired and won the treasure for us by his sufferings, death, and resurrection, etc. But if the work remained hidden and no one knew of it, it would have been all in vain, all lost. In order that this treasure might not be buried but put to use and enjoyed, God has caused the Word to be published and proclaimed, in which he has given the Holy Spirit to offer and apply to us this treasure of salvation. Therefore to sanctify is nothing else than to bring us to the Lord 39

---

[2] Christmas, Lent, Easter, Ascension.
[3] E.g., I Cor. 2:11.
[4] Cf. II Macc. 11:6, 15:23. Luther interpreted these as the good angels.
[5] Cf. I Sam. 16:14, 23; Tobit 3:8; Acts 19:12, 15.

Christ to receive this blessing, which we could not obtain by ourselves.

Learn this article, then, as clearly as possible. If you are asked, 40 What do you mean by the words, "I believe in the Holy Spirit"? you can answer, "I believe that the Holy Spirit makes me holy, as his name implies." How does he do this? By what means? Answer: 41 "Through the Christian church, the forgiveness of sins, the resurrection of the body, and the life everlasting." In the first place, he has a 42 unique community in the world. It is the mother that begets and bears every Christian through the Word of God. The Holy Spirit reveals and preaches that Word, and by it he illumines and kindles hearts so that they grasp and accept it, cling to it, and persevere in it.

Where he does not cause the Word to be preached and does not 43 awaken understanding in the heart, all is lost. This was the case under the papacy, where faith was entirely shoved under the bench and no one recognized Christ as the Lord, or the Holy Spirit as the Sanctifier. That is, no one believed that Christ is our Lord in the sense that he won for us this treasure without our works and merits and made us acceptable to the Father. What was lacking here? There was no 44 Holy Spirit present to reveal this truth and have it preached. Men and evil spirits there were, teaching us to obtain grace and be saved by our works. Therefore there was no Christian church. For where 45 Christ is not preached, there is no Holy Spirit to create, call, and gather the Christian church, and outside it no one can come to the Lord Christ. Let this suffice concerning the substance of this 46 article. But since various points in it are not quite clear to the common people, we shall run through them also.

The Creed calls the holy Christian church a *communio sanc-* 47 *torum,* "a communion of saints." Both expressions have the same meaning. In early times the latter phrase was missing,[6] and it is unintelligible in our translation. If it is to be rendered idiomatically, we must express it quite differently. The word *ecclesia* properly means an assembly. We, however, are accustomed to the term 48 *Kirche,* "church," by which simple folk understand not a group of people but a consecrated house or building. But the house should not be called a church except for the single reason that the group of people assembles there. For we who assemble select a special place and give the house its name by virtue of the assembly. Thus the word "church" (*Kirche*) really means nothing else than a common assembly; it is not of German but of Greek origin, like the word *ecclesia.* In that language the word is *kyria,* and in Latin *curia.*[7] In our mother tongue

---

[6] In 1519 Luther expressed the opinion that the expression "communion of saints" was a late addition to the Creed, in apposition to "holy catholic Church" (*WA,* 2:190). The earliest extant version of the Creed containing the phrase is that attributed to Bishop Nicetas of Remesiana (*ca.* 400 ?).

[7] Luther was mistaken. *Kirche* comes not from the Greek *kria* or *kyriake* but from the Celtic word *kyrk* (the circumscribed), related to the Latin

therefore it ought to be called "a Christian congregation or assembly," [8] or best and most clearly of all, "a holy Christian people." [9]

Likewise the word *communio,* which is appended, should not be [49] translated "communion" but "community." [1] It is nothing but a comment or interpretation by which someone wished to explain what the Christian church is. But some among us, who understand neither Latin nor German, have rendered this "communion of saints," although no German would use or understand such an expression. To speak idiomatically, we ought to say "a community of saints," that is, a community composed only of saints, or, still more clearly, "a holy community." This I say in order that the expression may be [50] understood; it has become so established in usage that it cannot well be uprooted, and it would be next to heresy to alter a word.

This is the sum and substance of this phrase: I believe that [51] there is on earth a little holy flock or community of pure saints under one head, Christ. It is called together by the Holy Spirit in one faith, mind, and understanding. It possesses a variety of gifts, yet is united in love without sect or schism. Of this community I also am a [52] part and member, a participant and co-partner[2] in all the blessings it possesses. I was brought to it by the Holy Spirit and incorporated into it through the fact that I have heard and still hear God's Word, which is the first step in entering it. Before we had advanced this far, we were entirely of the devil, knowing nothing of God and of Christ. Until the last day the Holy Spirit remains with the holy community [53] or Christian people. Through it he gathers us, using it to teach and preach the Word. By it he creates and increases sanctification, causing it daily to grow and become strong in the faith and in the fruits of the Spirit.

Further we believe that in this Christian church we have the [54] forgiveness of sins, which is granted through the holy sacraments and absolution as well as through all the comforting words of the entire Gospel. Toward forgiveness is directed everything that is to be preached concerning the sacraments and, in short, the entire Gospel and all the duties of Christianity. Forgiveness is needed constantly, for although God's grace has been won by Christ, and holiness has been wrought by the Holy Spirit through God's Word in the unity of

circus and *carcer.* Again, curia is related not to the Greek *kyria* but to *Quiris* (Roman citizen).
[8] *Eline christliche Gemeine oder Sammlung.* In the Bible Luther always translated *ekklesia* with *Gemeine* (cf. Matt. 16:18; Acts 19:39f.; I Cor. 1:2; Gal. 1:2).
[9] *Eline heilige Christenheit.* In the treatise, "On the Councils and the Churches" (1539), Luther urged substitution of *Christenheit* or *christliches Volk* for the "un-German" and "blind" word *Kirche. WA,* 50:624f.
[1] Not *Gemeinschaft* but *Gemeine.*
[2] Cf. I Cor. 1:9.

the Christian church, yet because we are encumbered with our flesh
we are never without sin.

Therefore everything in the Christian church is so ordered that   55
we may daily obtain full forgiveness of sins through the Word and
through signs[3] appointed to comfort and revive our consciences as
long as we live. Although we have sin, the Holy Spirit sees to it that
it does not harm us because we are in the Christian church, where there
is full forgiveness of sin. God forgives us, and we forgive, bear with,
and aid one another.

But outside the Christian church (that is, where the Gospel is   56
not) there is no forgiveness, and hence no holiness. Therefore, all
who seek to merit holiness through their works rather than through
the Gospel and the forgiveness of sin have expelled and separated
themselves from the church.

Meanwhile, since holiness has begun and is growing daily, we   57
await the time when our flesh will be put to death, will be buried with
all its uncleanness, and will come forth gloriously and arise to
complete and perfect holiness in a new, eternal life. Now we are   58
only halfway pure and holy. The Holy Spirit must continue to work
in us through the Word, daily granting forgiveness until we attain
to that life where there will be no more forgiveness. In that life are
only perfectly pure and holy people, full of goodness and righteousness,
completely freed from sin, death, and all evil, living in new, immortal,
and glorified bodies.

All this, then, is the office and work of the Holy Spirit, to   59
begin and daily to increase holiness on earth through these two means,
the Christian church and the forgiveness of sins. Then, when we pass
from this life, he will instantly perfect our holiness and will eternally
preserve us in it by means of the last two parts of this article.

The term "resurrection of the flesh," however, is not well   60
chosen. When we Germans hear the word *Fleisch* (flesh), we think no
farther than the butcher shop. Idiomatically we would say "resurrection
of the body." [4] However, this is not of great importance, as long as
the words are rightly understood.

---

[3] The sacraments.

[4] *Auferstehung des Leibs oder Leichnams.* In the early church, the word
sarkos (flesh) apparently was inserted deliberately to combat the Gnostic
tendency to assert that only the "spirit" was capable of being saved, that the
body or flesh was by nature evil. In his exposition of John 1:14 (*WA*, 10^I:
235) Luther wrote: "By 'flesh' we should understand the whole human
nature, body and soul, in the manner of the Scriptures, which call man
'flesh,' . . . and in the Creed we say, 'I believe in the resurrection of the
flesh,' i.e., 'of all men.' " Older English translations of the Creed also read
"resurrection of the flesh" until 1543, when in "The Necessary Doctrine and
Erudition for any Christian Man," issued by Henry VIII, "resurrection of
the body" was introduced.

This, then, is the article which must always remain in force. 61 Creation is past and redemption is accomplished, but the Holy Spirit carries on his work unceasingly until the last day. For this purpose he has appointed a community on earth, through which he speaks and does all his work. For he has not yet gathered together all his 62 Christian people, nor has he completed the granting of forgiveness. Therefore we believe in him who daily brings us into this community through the Word, and imparts, increases, and strengthens faith through the same Word and the forgiveness of sins. Then when his work has been finished and we abide in it, having died to the world and all evil, he will finally make us perfectly and eternally holy. We now wait in faith for this to be accomplished through the Word.

Here in the Creed you have the entire essence of God, his will, 63 and his work exquisitely depicted in very short but rich words. In them consists all our wisdom, which surpasses all the wisdom, understanding, and reason of men. Although the whole world has sought painstakingly to learn what God is and what he thinks and does, yet it has never succeeded in the least. But here you have everything in richest measure. In these three articles God himself has revealed 64 and opened to us the most profound depths of his fatherly heart, his sheer, unutterable love. He created us for this very purpose, to redeem and sanctify us. Moreover, having bestowed upon us everything in heaven and on earth, he has given us his Son and his Holy Spirit, through whom he brings us to himself. As we explained before, 65 we could never come to recognize the Father's favor and grace were it not for the Lord Christ, who is a mirror of the Father's heart. Apart from him we see nothing but an angry and terrible Judge. But neither could we know anything of Christ, had it not been revealed by the Holy Spirit.

These articles of the Creed, therefore, divide and distinguish us 66 Christians from all other people on earth. All who are outside the Christian church, whether heathen, Turks, Jews, or false Christians and hypocrites, even though they believe in and worship only the one, true God, nevertheless do not know what his attitude is toward them. They cannot be confident of his love and blessing. Therefore they remain in eternal wrath and damnation, for they do not have the Lord Christ, and, besides, they are not illuminated and blessed by the gifts of the Holy Spirit.

Now you see that the Creed is a very different teaching from 67 the Ten Commandments. The latter teach us what we ought to do; the Creed tells what God does for us and gives to us. The Ten Commandments, moreover, are inscribed in the hearts of all men.[5]

[5] Cf. Rom. 2:15. Luther was thinking of the natural law. See also above, Third Commandment, 82 and footnote.

No human wisdom can comprehend the Creed; it must be taught by the Holy Spirit alone. Therefore the Ten Commandments do not   68 by themselves make us Christians, for God's wrath and displeasure still remain on us because we cannot fulfill his demands. But the Creed brings pure grace and makes us upright and pleasing to God. Through this knowledge we come to love and delight in all the   69 commandments of God because we see that God gives himself completely to us, with all his gifts and his power, to help us keep the Ten Commandments: the Father gives us all creation, Christ all his works, the Holy Spirit all his gifts.

For the present this is enough concerning the Creed to lay a   70 foundation for the common people without overburdening them. After they understand the substance of it, they may on their own initiative learn more, relating to these teachings of the Catechism all that they learn in the Scriptures, and thus advance and grow richer in understanding. For as long as we live we shall have enough to preach and learn on the subject of faith.

THIRD PART: THE LORD'S PRAYER

We have heard what we are to do and believe. The best and most   1 blessed life consists of these things. Now follows the third part, how we are to pray. Mankind is in such a situation that no one can   2 keep the Ten Commandments perfectly, even though he has begun to believe. Besides, the devil, along with the world and our flesh, resists our efforts with all his power. Consequently nothing is so necessary as to call upon God incessantly and drum into his ears our prayer that he may give, preserve, and increase in us faith and obedience to the Ten Commandments and remove all that stands in our way and hinders us from fulfilling them. That we may know what and how to pray,   3 our Lord Christ himself has taught us both the way and the words, as we shall see.

Before we explain the Lord's Prayer part by part, it is very   4 necessary to exhort and draw the people to prayer, as Christ and the apostles also did.[6] The first thing to know is this: It is our duty to   5 pray because God has commanded it. We were told in the Second Commandment, "You shall not take God's name in vain." Thereby we are required to praise the holy name and pray or call upon it in every need. For to call upon it is nothing else than to pray. Prayer,   6 therefore, is as strictly and solemnly commanded as all the other commandments, such as having no other God, not killing, not stealing,

---

[6] Cf. Matt. 7:7; Luke 18:1, 21:36; Rom. 12:12; Col. 4:2; I Thess. 5:17; I Tim. 2:1; James 1:6, 5:13; I Pet. 4:8; Jude 20.

etc. Let no one think that it makes no difference whether I pray or not, as vulgar people do who say in their delusion: "Why should I pray? Who knows whether God heeds my prayer or cares to hear it? If I do not pray, someone else will." Thus they fall into the habit of never praying, alleging that since we reject false and hypocritical prayers we teach that there is no duty or need to pray.

It is quite true that the kind of babbling and bellowing that used   7 to pass for prayers in the church was not really prayer. Such external repetition, when properly used, may serve as an exercise for young children, pupils, and simple folk; while it may be called singing or reading exercise, it is not real prayer. To pray, as the Second   8 Commandment teaches, is to call upon God in every need. This God requires of us; he has not left it to our choice. It is our duty and obligation to pray if we want to be Christians, just as it is our duty and obligation to obey our fathers and mothers and the civil authorities. By invocation and prayer the name of God is glorified and used to good purpose. This you should note above all, so that you may silence and repel any thoughts that would prevent or deter us from praying. It would be improper for a son to say to his father: "What is the use   9 of being obedient? I will go and do as I please; what difference does it make?" But there stands the commandment, "You shall and must obey!" Just so, it is not left to my choice here whether to pray or not, but it is my duty and obligation [on pain of God's wrath and displeasure].[7]

[This should be kept in mind above all things so that you may   10 silence and repel thoughts which would prevent or deter us from praying, as though it made no great difference if we do not pray, or as though prayer were commanded for those who are holier and in better favor with God than we are. Indeed, the human heart is by nature so desperately wicked that it always flees from God, thinking that he neither wants nor cares for our prayers because we are sinners and have merited nothing but wrath. Against such thoughts, I say, we   11 should respect this commandment and turn to God so that we may not provoke his anger by such disobedience. By this commandment he makes it clear that he will not cast us out or drive us away, even though we are sinners; he wishes rather to draw us to himself so that we may humble ourselves before him, lament our misery and plight, and pray for grace and help. Therefore we read in the Scriptures that he is angry because those who were struck down for their sin did not return to him and assuage his wrath and seek grace by their prayers.]

[7] The text in square brackets here and in the following paragraph (sections 10, 11) does not appear in the first edition of the Large Catechism, in the Jena edition of Luther's works, or in the 1580 German edition of the Book of Concord. It is found in revised editions of the Catechism (1529 and later), in the Latin translation of 1544, and freshly translated in the Latin Book of Concord, 1584.

From the fact that prayer is so urgently commanded, we ought   12
to conclude that we should by no means despise our prayers, but
rather prize them highly. Take an illustration from the other commandments. A child should never despise obedience to his father   13
and mother, but should always reflect: "This is a work of obedience,
and what I do has no other purpose than that it befits obedience and
the commandment of God. On this I can rely and depend, and I can
revere it highly, not because of my worthiness, but because of the
commandment." So, too, here. What we shall pray, and for what, we
should regard as demanded by God and done in obedience to him.
We should think, "On my account this prayer would amount to
nothing; but it is important because God has commanded it." So, no
matter what he has to pray for, everybody should always approach God
in obedience to this commandment.

We therefore urgently beg and exhort everyone to take these   14
words to heart and in no case to despise prayer. Prayer used to be
taught, in the devil's name, in such a way that no one paid any
attention to it, and men supposed it was enough if the act was
performed, whether God heard it or not. But that is to stake prayer
on luck and to mumble aimlessly. Such a prayer is worthless.

We allow ourselves to be hindered and deterred by such   15
thoughts as these: "I am not holy enough or worthy enough; if I were
as godly and holy as St. Peter or St. Paul, then I would pray." Away
with such thoughts! The very commandment that applied to St. Paul
applies also to me. The Second Commandment is given just as much
on my account as on his. He can boast of no better or holier
commandment than I.

Therefore you should say: "The prayer I offer is just as   16
precious, holy, and pleasing to God as those of St. Paul and the holiest
of saints. The reason is this: I freely admit that he is holier in respect
to his person, but not on account of the commandment. God does not
regard prayer on account of the person, but on account of his Word
and the obedience accorded it. On this commandment, on which all
the saints base their prayer, I, too, base mine. Moreover, I pray for
the same thing for which they all pray, or ever have prayed." [8]

This is the first and most important point, that all our prayers   17
must be based on obedience to God, regardless of our person, whether
we be ṣinners or saints, worthy or unworthy. We must learn that   18
God will not have this commandment treated as a jest but will be
angry and punish us if we do not pray, just as he punishes all other
kinds of disobedience. Nor will he allow our prayers to be frustrated
or lost, for if he did not intend to answer you, he would not have

---

[8] Later edition adds: And I have just as great a need for it as those great
saints—indeed, a greater need than they.

ordered you to pray and backed it up with such a strict commandment.

In the second place, we should be all the more urged and 19
encouraged to pray because God has promised that our prayer will
surely be answered, as he says in Ps. 50:15, "Call upon me in the day
of trouble, and I will deliver you," and Christ says in Matt. 7:7, 8, "Ask
and it will be given you," etc. "For every one who asks receives."
Such promises certainly ought to awaken and kindle in our hearts 20
a desire and love to pray. For by his Word God testifies that our
prayer is heartily pleasing to him and will assuredly be heard and
granted, so that we may not despise or disdain it or pray uncertainly.

This you can hold up to him and say, "I come to Thee, dear 21
Father, and pray not of my own accord or because of my own
worthiness, but at thy commandment and promise, which cannot fail
or deceive me." Whoever does not believe this promise should realize
once again that he angers God, grossly dishonoring him and accusing
him of falsehood.

Furthermore, we should be encouraged and drawn to pray 22
because, in addition to this commandment and promise, God takes the
initiative and puts into our mouths the very words we are to use
Thus we see how sincerely he is concerned over our needs, and we
shall never doubt that our prayer pleases him and will assuredly be
heard. So this prayer is far superior to all others that we might 23
ourselves devise. For in the latter our conscience would always be in
doubt, saying, "I have prayed, but who knows whether it pleased him,
or whether I have hit upon the right form and mode?" Thus there
is no nobler prayer to be found on earth,[9] for it has the excellent
testimony that God loves to hear it. This we should not trade for all
the riches in the world.

It has been prescribed for this reason, also, that we should 24
reflect on our needs, which ought to drive and impel us to pray
without ceasing. A person who wants to pray must present a petition,
naming and asking for something which he desires; otherwise it
cannot be called a prayer.

Therefore we have rightly rejected the prayers of monks and 25
priests, who howl and growl frightfully day and night; not one of them
thinks of asking for the least thing. If we gathered all the churches
together, with all their clergy, they would have to confess that they
never prayed whole-heartedly for so much as a drop of wine. None
of them has ever undertaken to pray out of obedience to God and faith
in his promise, or out of consideration for his own needs. They only
thought, at best, of doing a good work as a payment to God, not
willing to receive anything from him, but only to give him something.

But where there is true prayer there must be earnestness. We 26

[9] Later edition adds: than the daily Lord's Prayer.

must feel our need, the distress that impels and drives us to cry out.
Then prayer will come spontaneously, as it should, and we shall not
need to be taught how to prepare for it or how to generate devotion.
The need which ought to be the concern of both ourselves and   27
others is quite amply indicated in the Lord's Prayer. Therefore it may
serve to remind us and impress upon us not to become negligent about
praying. We all have needs enough, but the trouble is that we do not
feel or see them. God therefore wishes you to lament and express
your needs and wants, not because he is unaware of them, but in order
that you may kindle your heart to stronger and greater desires and
spread your cloak wide to receive many things.

Each of us should form the habit from his youth up to pray   28
daily for all his needs, whenever he is aware of anything that affects
him or other people around him, such as preachers, magistrates,
neighbors, servants; and, as we have said, he should always remind
God of his commandment and promise, knowing that he will not have
them despised. This I say because I would like to see the people   29
brought again to pray rightly and not act so crudely and coldly that
they become daily more inept at praying. This is just what the devil
wants and works for with all his might, for he is well aware what
damage and harm he suffers when prayer is in proper use.

This we must know, that all our safety and protection consist   30
in prayer alone. We are far too weak to cope with the devil and all
his might and his forces arrayed against us, trying to trample us under
foot. Therefore we must carefully select the weapons with which
Christians ought to arm themselves in order to stand against the devil.
What do you think has accomplished such great results in the   31
past, parrying the counsels and plots of our enemies and checking
their murderous and seditious designs by which the devil expected to
crush us, and the Gospel as well, except that the prayers of a few
godly men intervened like an iron wall on our side? Otherwise they
would have witnessed a far different drama: the devil would have
destroyed all Germany in its own blood. Now they may confidently
ridicule and mock. But by prayer alone we shall be a match both for
them and for the devil, if we only persevere diligently and do not
become slack. For whenever a good Christian prays, "Dear   32
Father, thy will be done," God replies from on high, "Yes, dear child,
it shall indeed be done in spite of the devil and all the world."

Let this be said as an admonition in order that men may learn   33
above all to value prayer as a great and precious thing and may clearly
distinguish between vain babbling and praying for something definite.
We by no means reject prayer, but we do denounce the utterly useless
howling and growling, as Christ himself rejects and forbids great

wordiness.[1] Now we shall treat the Lord's Prayer very briefly and   34
clearly. In seven successive articles or petitions are comprehended
all the needs that continually beset us, each one so great that it should
impel us to keep praying for it all our lives.

THE FIRST PETITION

"Hallowed be thy name."   35
This is rather obscure. It is not idiomatic German. In our   36
mother tongue we would say, "Heavenly Father, grant that thy name
alone may be holy." But what is it to pray that his name may   37
become holy? Is it not already holy? Answer: Yes, in itself it is
holy, but not in our use of it. God's name was given to us when we
became Christians at Baptism, and so we are called children of God
and enjoy the sacraments, through which he so incorporates us with
himself that all that is God's must serve for our use.

So we should realize that we are under the great necessity of   38
duly honoring his name and keeping it holy and sacred, regarding it
as the greatest treasure and most sacred thing we have, and praying,
as good children, that his name, which is already holy in heaven, may
also be kept holy on earth by us and all the world.

How does it become holy among us? The plainest answer is: 39
When both our teaching and our life are godly and Christian. Since in
this prayer we call God our Father, it is our duty in every way to
behave as good children so that he may receive from us not shame
but honor and praise.

Now, the name of God is profaned by us either in words or in   40
deeds; everything we do on earth may be classified as word or deed,
speech or act. In the first place, then, it is profaned when men   41
preach, teach, and speak in God's name anything that is false and
deceptive, using his name to cloak lies and make them acceptable; this
is the worst profanation and dishonor of the divine name. Like-   42
wise, when men grossly misuse the divine name as a cloak for their
shame, by swearing, cursing, conjuring, etc. In the next place, it is   43
also profaned by an openly evil life and wicked works, when those
who are called Christians and God's people are adulterers, drunkards,
gluttons, jealous persons, and slanderers. Here again God's name must
be profaned and blasphemed because of us.

Just as it is a shame and disgrace to an earthly father to have   44
a bad, unruly child who antagonizes him in word and deed with the
result that on his account the father suffers scorn and reproach, so God
is dishonored if we who are called by his name and enjoy his manifold
blessings fail to teach, speak, and live as godly and heavenly children

[1] Matt. 6:7, 23:14.

with the result that he must hear us called not children of God but children of the devil.

So you see that in this petition we pray for exactly the same 45 thing that God demands in the Second Commandment: that his name should not be taken in vain by swearing, cursing, deceiving, etc., but used rightly to the praise and glory of God. Whoever uses God's name for any sort of wrong profanes and desecrates this holy name, as in the past a church was said to be desecrated when a murder or any other crime had been committed in it, or when a monstrance[2] or a relic was profaned, thus rendering unholy by misuse that which is holy in itself. This petition, then, is simple and clear as soon as we understand 46 the language, namely, that "to hallow" means the same as in our idiom "to praise, extol, and honor" in word and deed.

See, then, what a great need there is for this kind of prayer! 47 Since we see that the world is full of sects and false teachers, all of whom wear the holy name as a cloak and warrant for their devilish doctrine, we ought constantly to cry out against all who preach and believe falsely and against those who attack and persecute our Gospel and pure doctrine and try to suppress it, as the bishops, tyrants, fanatics, and others do. Likewise, this petition is for ourselves who have the Word of God but are ungrateful for it and fail to live according to it as we ought. If you pray the petition whole-heartedly, you can be 48 sure that God is pleased. For there is nothing he would rather hear than to have his glory and praise exalted above everything else and his Word taught in its purity and cherished and treasured.

The Second Petition

"Thy kingdom come."

We prayed in the first petition that God would prevent the 49 world from using his glory and name to cloak its lies and wickedness, but would rather keep God's name sacred and holy in both doctrine and life so that he may be praised and exalted in us. Here we ask that his kingdom may come. Just as God's name is holy in itself 50 and yet we pray that it may be holy among us, so also his kingdom comes of itself without our prayer and yet we pray that it may come to us. That is, we ask that it may prevail among us and with us, so that we may be a part of those among whom his name is hallowed and his kingdom flourishes.

What is the kingdom of God? Answer: Simply what we learned 51 in the Creed, namely, that God sent his Son, Christ our Lord, into the world to redeem and deliver us from the power of the devil and to bring us to himself and rule us as a king of righteousness, life, and

---

[2] The monstrance was the vessel in which the host was displayed for adoration.

salvation against sin, death, and an evil conscience. To this end he also gave his Holy Spirit to teach us this through his holy Word and to enlighten and strengthen us in faith by his power.

We pray here at the outset that all this may be realized in us 52 and that God's name may be praised through his holy Word and our Christian lives. This we ask, both in order that we who have accepted it may remain faithful and grow daily in it and in order that it may gain recognition and followers among other people and advance with power throughout the world. So we pray that, led by the Holy Spirit, many may come into the kingdom of grace and become partakers of salvation, so that we may all remain together eternally in this kingdom which has now made its appearance among us.

God's kingdom comes to us in two ways: first, it comes here, in 53 time, through the Word and faith, and secondly, in eternity, it comes through the final revelation.[3] Now, we pray for both of these, that it may come to those who are not yet in it, and that it may come by daily growth here and in eternal life hereafter to us who have attained it. All this is simply to say: "Dear Father, we pray Thee, give us thy 54 Word, that the Gospel may be sincerely preached throughout the world and that it may be received by faith and may work and live in us. So we pray that thy kingdom may prevail among us through the Word and the power of the Holy Spirit, that the devil's kingdom may be overthrown and he may have no right or power over us, until finally the devil's kingdom shall be utterly destroyed and sin, death, and hell exterminated, and that we may live forever in perfect righteousness and blessedness."

You see that we are praying here not for a crust of bread or 55 for a temporal, perishable blessing, but for an eternal, priceless treasure and everything that God himself possesses. It would be far too great for any human heart to dare to desire if God himself had not commanded us to ask for it. But because he is God, he claims 56 the honor of giving far more abundantly and liberally than anyone can comprehend—like an eternal, inexhaustible fountain which, the more it gushes forth and overflows, the more it continues to give. He desires of us nothing more ardently than that we ask many and great things of him; and on the contrary, he is angered if we do not ask and demand confidently.

Imagine a very rich and mighty emperor who bade a poor 57 beggar to ask for whatever he might desire and was prepared to give great and princely gifts, and the fool asked only for a dish of beggar's broth. He would rightly be considered a rogue and a scoundrel who had made a mockery of his imperial majesty's command and was unworthy to come into his presence. Just so, it is a great reproach

---

[3] I.e., the return of Christ.

and dishonor to God if we, to whom he offers and pledges so many inexpressible blessings, despise them or lack confidence that we shall receive them and scarcely venture to ask for a morsel of bread.

The fault lies wholly in that shameful unbelief which does not 58 look to God even for enough to satisfy the belly, let alone expect, without doubting, eternal blesings from God. Therefore we must strengthen ourselves against unbelief and let the kingdom of God be the first thing for which we pray. Then, surely, we shall have all the other things in abundance, as Christ teaches, "Seek first the kingdom of God, and all these things shall be yours as well." [4] For how could God allow us to suffer want in temporal things when he promises that which is eternal and imperishable?

THE THIRD PETITION

"Thy will be done on earth, as it is in heaven."   59

Thus far we have prayed that God's name may be hallowed by 60 us and that his kingdom may prevail among us. These two points embrace all that pertains to God's glory and to our salvation, in which we appropriate God with all his treasures. But there is just as great need that we keep firm hold of these two things and never allow ourselves to be torn from them. In a good government there is 61 need not only for good builders and rulers, but also for defenders, protectors, and vigilant guardians. So here also; although we have prayed for what is most essential—for the Gospel, for faith, and for the Holy Spirit, that he may govern us who have been redeemed from the power of the devil—we must also pray that God's will may be done. If we try to hold fast these treasures, we must suffer an astonishing amount of attacks and assaults from all who venture to hinder and thwart the fulfillment of the first two petitions.

It is unbelievable how the devil opposes and obstructs their 62 fulfillment. He cannot bear to have anyone teach or believe rightly. It pains him beyond measure when his lies and abominations, honored under the most specious pretexts of God's name, are disclosed and exposed in all their shame, when he himself is driven out of men's hearts and a breach is made in his kingdom. Therefore, like a furious foe, he raves and rages with all his power and might, marshaling all his subjects and even enlisting the world and our own flesh as his allies. For our flesh is in itself vile and inclined to evil, even when 63 we have accepted and believe God's Word. The world, too, is perverse and wicked. These he stirs up, fanning and feeding the flames, in order to hinder us, put us to flight, cut us down, and bring us once more under his power. This is his only purpose, his desire and 64

---

[4] Matt. 6:33.

thought. For this end he strives without rest day and night, using all the arts, tricks, ways, and means that he can devise.

Therefore we who would be Christians must surely count on 65 having the devil with all his angels[5] and the world as our enemies and must count on their inflicting every possible misfortune and grief upon us. For where God's Word is preached, accepted or believed, and bears fruit, there the blessed holy cross will not be far away. Let nobody think that he will have peace; he must sacrifice all he has on earth—possessions, honor, house and home, wife and children, body and life. Now, this grieves our flesh and the old Adam, for it 66 means that we must remain steadfast, suffer patiently whatever befalls us, and let go whatever is taken from us.

Therefore, there is just as much need in this case as in every 67 other case to pray without ceasing: "Thy will be done, dear Father, and not the will of the devil or of our enemies, nor of those who would persecute and suppress thy holy Word or prevent thy kingdom from coming; and grant that whatever we must suffer on its account, we may patiently bear and overcome, so that our poor flesh may not yield or fall away through weakness or indolence."

Observe that in these three petitions interests which concern 68 God himself have been very simply expressed, yet we have prayed in our own behalf. What we pray for concerns only ourselves when we ask that what otherwise must be done without us may also be done in us. As God's name must be hallowed and his kingdom must come even without our prayer, so must his will be done and prevail even though the devil and all his host storm and rage furiously against it in their attempt utterly to exterminate the Gospel. But for our own sake we must pray that his will may be done among us without hindrance, in spite of their fury, so that they may accomplish nothing and we may remain steadfast in the face of all violence and persecution, submitting to the will of God.

Such prayer must be our protection and defense now to repulse 69 and beat down all that the devil,[6] bishops, tyrants, and heretics can do against our Gospel. Let them all rage and do their worst, let them plot and plan how to suppress and exterminate us so that their will and scheme may prevail. One or two Christians, armed with this single petition, shall be our bulwark, against which the others shall dash themselves to pieces. It is our solace and boast that the will and 70 purpose of the devil and of all our enemies shall and must fail and come to naught, no matter how proud, secure, and powerful they think they are. For if their will were not broken and frustrated, the kingdom of God could not abide on earth nor his name be hallowed.

[5] On the devil's angels, cf. Matt. 25:41.
[6] Later version adds: pope.

THE FOURTH PETITION

"Give us this day our daily bread."   71

Here we consider the poor bread-basket—the needs of our body   72
and our life on earth. It is a brief and simple word, but very
comprehensive. When you pray for "daily bread" you pray for everything that is necessary in order to have and enjoy daily bread and, on
the contrary, against everything that interferes with enjoying it. You
must therefore enlarge and extend your thoughts to include not only
the oven or the flour bin, but also the broad fields and the whole land
which produce and provide for us our daily bread and all kinds of
sustenance. For if God did not cause grain to grow and did not
bless and preserve it in the field, we could never take a loaf of bread
from the oven to set on the table.

To put it briefly, this petition includes everything that belongs   73
to our entire life in this world; only for its sake do we need daily bread.
Now, our life requires not only food and clothing and other necessities
for our body, but also peace and concord in our daily business and
in associations of every description with the people among whom we
live and move—in short, everything that pertains to the regulation of
our domestic and our civil or political affairs. For where these two
relations are interfered with and prevented from functioning properly,
there the necessities of life are also interfered with, and life itself cannot
be maintained for any length of time. Indeed, the greatest need of   74
all is to pray for our civil authorities and the government, for chiefly
through them does God provide us our daily bread and all the comforts
of this life. Although we have received from God all good things in
abundance, we cannot retain any of them or enjoy them in security
and happiness unless he gives us a stable, peaceful government. For
where dissension, strife, and war prevail, there our daily bread is taken
away, or at least reduced.

It would therefore be fitting if the coat-of-arms of every upright   75
prince were emblazoned with a loaf of bread instead of a lion or a
wreath of rue, or if a loaf of bread were stamped on coins, to remind
both princes and subjects that through the office of the princes we
enjoy protection and peace and that without them we could not have
the steady blessing of daily bread.[7] Rulers are worthy of all honor,
and we should render them the duties we owe and do all we can for
them, as to those through whom we enjoy our possessions in peace
and quietness, since otherwise we could not keep a penny. Moreover,
we should pray for them, that through them God may bestow on us
still more blessings and good things.

---

[7] A black lion on gold appeared on the coat-of-arms of the March of
Meissen, a red and white striped lion on blue on that of the County of
Thuringia, a wreath of rue on that of Electoral Saxony. The *Löwenpfennig*
of Saxony and of Brunswick showed a lion on the coat-of-arms.

Let us outline very briefly how comprehensively this petition 76 covers all kinds of relations on earth. Out of it one might make a long prayer, enumerating with many words all the things it includes. For example, we might ask God to give us food and drink, clothing, house, home, and a sound body; to cause the grain and fruits of the field to grow and yield richly; to help us manage our household well and give and preserve to us a good wife, children, and servants; to cause our work, craft, or occupation, whatever it may be, to prosper and succeed; to grant us faithful neighbors and good friends, etc. Again, to ask God to endow the emperor, kings, and all estates of 77 men, and especially our princes, counselors, magistrates, and officials, with wisdom, strength, and prosperity to govern well and to be victorious over the Turks and all our enemies; to grant their subjects and the people at large to live together in obedience, peace, and concord. On the other hand, to protect us from all kinds of harm 78 to our body and our livelihood, from tempest, hail, fire, and flood; from poison, pestilence, and cattle-plague; from war and bloodshed, famine, savage beasts, wicked men, etc. It is good to impress upon 79 the common people that all these things come from God and that we must pray for them.

But especially is this petition directed against our chief enemy, 80 the devil, whose whole purpose and desire it is to take away or interfere with all we have received from God. He is not satisfied to obstruct and overthrow spiritual order, so that he may deceive men with his lies and bring them under his power, but he also prevents and hinders the establishment of any kind of government or honorable and peaceful relations on earth. This is why he causes so much contention, murder, sedition, and war, why he sends tempest and hail to destroy crops and cattle, why he poisons the air, etc. In short, 81 it pains him that anyone receives a morsel of bread from God and eats it in peace. If it were in his power, and our prayer to God did not restrain him, surely we would not have a straw in the field, a penny in the house, or even our life for one hour—especially those of us who have the Word of God and would like to be Christians.

Thus, you see, God wishes to show us how he cares for us in 82 all our needs and faithfully provides for our daily existence. Although he gives and provides these blessings bountifully, even 83 for wicked men and rogues, yet he wishes us to pray for them so we may realize that we have received them from his hand and may recognize in them his fatherly goodness toward us. When he withdraws his hand, nothing can prosper or last for any length of time, as indeed we see and experience every day. How much trouble there now 84 is in the world simply on account of false coinage, yes, on account of daily exploitation and usury in public business, trading, and labor on the part of those who wantonly oppress the poor and deprive them of

their daily bread! This we must put up with, of course; but let
exploiters and oppressors beware lest they lose the common intercession
of the church,[8] and let them take care lest this petition of the Lord's
Prayer be turned against them.

THE FIFTH PETITION

"And forgive us our debts, as we forgive our debtors."   85

This petition has to do with our poor, miserable life. Although   86
we have God's Word and believe, although we obey and submit to
his will and are supported by God's gift and blessing, nevertheless we
are not without sin. We still stumble daily and transgress because
we live in the world among people who sorely vex us and give us
occasion for impatience, wrath, vengeance, etc. Besides, Satan is   87
at our backs, besieging us on every side and, as we have heard,
directing his attacks against all the previous petitions, so that it is not
possible always to stand firm in such a ceaseless conflict.

Here again there is great need to call upon God and pray,   88
"Dear Father, forgive us our debts." Not that he does not forgive sin
even without and before our prayer; and he gave us the Gospel, in
which there is nothing but forgiveness, before we prayed or even
thought of it. But the point here is for us to recognize and accept this
forgiveness. For the flesh in which we daily live is of such a   89
nature that it does not trust and believe God and is constantly aroused
by evil desires and devices, so that we sin daily in word and deed, in
acts of commission and omission. Thus our conscience becomes
restless; it fears God's wrath and displeasure, and so it loses the
comfort and confidence of the Gospel. Therefore it is necessary
constantly to turn to this petition for the comfort that will restore our
conscience.

This should serve God's purpose to break our pride and keep   90
us humble. He has reserved to himself this prerogative, that if anybody
boasts of his goodness and despises others he should examine himself
in the light of this petition. He will find that he is no better than others,
that in the presence of God all men must humble themselves and be
glad that they can attain forgiveness. Let no one think that he   91
will ever in this life reach the point where he does not need this
forgiveness. In short, unless God constantly forgives, we are lost.

Thus this petition is really an appeal to God not to regard our   92
sins and punish us as we daily deserve, but to deal graciously with us,
forgive as he has promised, and thus grant us a happy and cheerful
conscience to stand before him in prayer. Where the heart is not right
with God and cannot achieve such confidence, it will never dare to

[8] The general prayer in the church. This was a kind of proverbial
expression, meaning "lose public respect."

pray. But such a confident and joyful heart can only come from the knowledge that our sins are forgiven.

Meanwhile, a necessary but comforting clause is added, "as we 93 forgive our debtors." God has promised us assurance that everything is forgiven and pardoned, yet on the condition that we also forgive our neighbor. Inasmuch as we sin greatly against God everyday 94 and yet he forgives it all through grace, we must always forgive our neighbor who does us harm, violence, and injustice, bears malice toward us, etc. If you do not forgive, do not think that God 95 forgives you. But if you forgive, you have the comfort and assurance that you are forgiven in heaven. Not on account of your forgiving, 96 for God does it altogether freely, out of pure grace, because he has promised it, as the Gospel teaches. But he has set up this condition for our strengthening and assurance as a sign along with the promise which is in agreement with this petition, Luke 6:37, "Forgive, and you will be forgiven." Therefore Christ repeats it immediately after the Lord's Prayer in Matt. 6:14, saying, "If you forgive men their trespasses, your heavenly Father also will forgive you," etc.

This sign is attached to the petition, therefore, that when we 97 pray we may recall the promise and think, "Dear Father, I come to Thee praying for forgiveness, not because I can make satisfaction or merit anything by my works, but because Thou hast given the promise and hast set thy seal to it, making it as certain as an absolution pronounced by thyself." Whatever can be effected by Baptism 98 and the Lord's Supper, which are appointed as outward signs, this sign also can effect to strengthen and gladden our conscience. And it has been especially instituted for us to use and practice every hour, keeping it with us at all times.

THE SIXTH PETITION

"And lead us not into temptation." 99

We have now heard enough about the trouble and effort 100 required to retain and persevere in all the gifts for which we pray. This, however, is not accomplished without failures and stumbling. Moreover, although we have acquired forgiveness and a good conscience, and have been wholly absolved, yet such is life that one stands today and falls tomorrow. Therefore, even though at present we are upright and stand before God with a good conscience, we must pray again that he will not allow us to fall and yield to trials and temptations.

Temptation (or, as the ancient Saxons called it, *Bekörunge*)[9] 101 is of three kinds: of the flesh, the world, and the devil. We live 102

[9] By Saxony Luther meant Lower Saxony; in the sixteenth century *Plattdeutsch* was spoken in Wittenberg. In the Latin Book of Concord *Bekörunge* was misunderstood as *Bekehrung, conversio*.

in the flesh and we have the old Adam hanging around our necks; he goes to work and lures us daily into unchastity, laziness, gluttony and drunkenness, greed and deceit, into acts of fraud and deception against our neighbor—in short, into all kinds of evil lusts which by nature cling to us and to which we are incited by the association and example of other people and by things we hear and see. All this often wounds and inflames even an innocent heart.

Next comes the world, which assails us by word and deed and   103 drives us to anger and impatience. In short, there is in it nothing but hatred and envy, enmity, violence and injustice, perfidy, vengeance, cursing, reviling, slander, arrogance, and pride, along with fondness for luxury, honor, fame, and power. No one is willing to be the least, but everyone wants to sit in the chief seat and be seen by all.

Then comes the devil, who baits and badgers us on all sides,   104 but especially exerts himself where the conscience and spiritual matters are at stake. His purpose is to make us scorn and despise both the Word and the works of God, to tear us away from faith, hope, and love, to draw us into unbelief, false security, and stubbornness, or, on the contrary, to drive us into despair, atheism, blasphemy, and countless other abominable sins. These are snares and nets; indeed, they are the real "flaming darts" [1] which are venomously shot into our hearts, not by flesh and blood but by the devil.

These are the great, grievous perils and temptations which   105 every Christian must bear, even if they come one by one. As long as we remain in this vile life in which we are attacked, hunted, and harried on all sides, we are constrained to cry out and pray every hour that God may not allow us to become faint and weary and to fall back into sin, shame, and unbelief. Otherwise it is impossible to overcome even the least temptation.

This, then, is "leading us not into temptation" when God   106 gives us power and strength to resist, even though the tribulation is not removed or ended. For no one can escape temptations and allurements as long as we live in the flesh and have the devil prowling about us. We cannot help but suffer tribulations, and even be entangled in them, but we pray here that we may not fall into them and be overwhelmed by them.

To feel temptation, therefore, is quite a different thing from   107 consenting and yielding to it. We must all feel it, though not all to the same degree; some have more frequent and severe temptations than others. Youths, for example, are tempted chiefly by the flesh; older people are tempted by the world. Others, who are concerned with spiritual matters (that is, strong Christians) are tempted by the devil. But we cannot be harmed by the mere feeling of temptation as   108

[1] Cf. Eph. 6:16.

long as it is contrary to our will and and we would prefer to be rid of it. If we did not feel it, it could not be called a temptation. But to consent to it is to give it free rein and neither resist it nor pray for help against it.

Accordingly we Christians must be armed and prepared for 109 incessant attacks. Then we shall not go about securely and heedlessly as if the devil were far from us but shall at all times expect his blows and parry them. Even if at present I am chaste, patient, kind, and firm in faith, the devil is likely in this very hour to send such a shaft into my heart that I can scarcely stand, for he is an enemy who never stops or becomes weary; when one attack ceases, new ones always arise.

At such times your only help or comfort is to take refuge in 110 the Lord's Prayer and to appeal to God from your heart, "Dear Father, Thou hast commanded me to pray; let me not fall because of tempta- tion." Then you will see the temptation cease and eventually 111 admit defeat. Otherwise, if you attempt to help yourself by your own thoughts and counsels, you will only make the matter worse and give the devil a better opening. For he has a serpent's head; if it finds an opening into which it can slip, the whole body will irresistibly follow. But prayer can resist him and drive him back.

THE LAST PETITION

"But deliver us from evil. Amen."   112

In the Greek[2] this petition reads, "Deliver or keep us from 113 the Evil One, or the Wicked One." The petition seems to be speaking of the devil as the sum of all evil in order that the entire substance of our prayer may be directed against our arch-enemy. It is he who obstructs everything that we pray for: God's name or glory, God's kingdom and will, our daily bread, a good and cheerful conscience, etc.

Therefore we sum it all up by saying, "Dear Father, help us to 114 get rid of all this misfortune." Nevertheless, this petition includes 115 all the evil that may befall us under the devil's kingdom: poverty, shame, death, and, in short, all the tragic misery and heartache of which there is so incalculably much on earth. Since the devil is not only a liar but also a murderer,[3] he incessantly seeks our life and vents his anger by causing accidents and injury to our bodies. He breaks many a man's neck and drives others to insanity; some he drowns, and many he hounds to suicide or other dreadful catastrophes. Therefore there is nothing for us to do on earth but to pray 116 constantly against this arch-enemy. For if God did not support us, we would not be safe from him for a single hour.

---

[2] The first edition of the Large Catechism reads erroneously, "In the Hebrew."

[3] John 8:44.

Thus you see how God wants us to pray to him for every- | 17
thing that affects our bodily welfare and directs us to seek and expect
help from no one but him. But this petition he has put last, for | 18
if we are to be protected and delivered from all evil, his name must
first be hallowed in us, his kingdom come among us, and his will be
done. Then he will preserve us from sin and shame and from everything else that harms or injures us.

Thus God has briefly set before us all the afflictions that may | 19
ever beset us in order that we may never have an excuse for failing
to pray. But the efficacy of prayer consists in our learning also to say
"Amen" to it—that is, not to doubt that our prayer is surely heard and
will be granted. This word is nothing else than an unquestioning 120
affirmation of faith on the part of one who does not pray as a matter of
chance but knows that God does not lie since he has promised to grant
his requests. Where such faith is wanting, there can be no true prayer.

It is therefore a pernicious delusion when people pray in such | 21
a way that they dare not whole-heartedly add "yes" and conclude with
certainty that God hears their prayer but remain in doubt, saying,
"Why should I be so bold as to boast that God hears my prayer? I am
only a poor sinner," etc. That means that they have their eye 122
not on God's promise but on their own works and worthiness, so that
they despise God and accuse him of lying. Therefore they receive | 23
nothing, as St. James says, "If anyone prays, let him ask in faith, with
no doubting, for he who doubts is like a wave of the sea that is driven
and tossed by the wind. For that person must not suppose that he
will receive anything from God." [4] Behold, such is the impor- | 24
tance that God attaches to our being certain that we do not pray in
vain and that we must not in any way despise our prayers.

FOURTH PART: BAPTISM

We have now finished with the three chief parts[5] of our common |
Christian teaching. It remains for us to speak of our two sacraments,
instituted by Christ. Every Christian ought to have at least some brief,
elementary instruction in them because without these no one can be
a Christian, although unfortunately in the past nothing was taught
about them. First we shall take up Baptism, through which we 2
are first received into the Christian community. In order that it may
be readily understood, we shall treat it in a systematic way and confine
ourselves to that which is necessary for us to know. How it is to be

---

[4] James 1:6, 7.

[5] Luther used the word *Hauptstücke* in a double sense: "major divisions"
but also "chief articles" or "the most essential." Cf. above, Large Catechism,
II, 6, and Small Catechism, VI, 8.

maintained and defended against heretics and sectarians we shall leave to the learned.

In the first place, we must above all be familiar with the words   3 upon which Baptism is founded and to which everything is related that is to be said on the subject, namely, where the Lord Christ says in Matt. 28:19,

"Go into all the world, and teach all nations, baptizing them in   4 the name of the Father and of the Son and of the Holy Spirit."

Likewise in Mark 16:16,

"He who believes and is baptized will be saved; but he who   5 does not believe will be condemned."

Observe, first, that these words contain God's commandment   6 and ordinance. You should not doubt, then, that Baptism is of divine origin, not something devised or invented by men. As truly as I can say that the Ten Commandments, the Creed, and the Lord's Prayer are not spun out of any man's imagination but revealed and given by God himself, so I can also boast that Baptism is no human plaything but is instituted by God himself. Moreover, it is solemnly and strictly commanded that we must be baptized or we shall not be saved. We are not to regard it as an indifferent matter, then, like putting on a new red coat. It is of the greatest importance that we regard   7 Baptism as excellent, glorious, and exalted. It is the chief cause of our contentions and battles because the world now is full of sects who proclaim that Baptism is an external thing and that external things are of no use.[6] But no matter how external it may be, here stand   8 God's Word and command which have instituted, established, and confirmed Baptism. What God institutes and commands cannot be useless. It is a most precious thing, even though to all appearances it may not be worth a straw. If people used to consider it a great   9 thing when the pope dispensed indulgences with his letters and bulls and consecrated altars and churches solely by virtue of his letters and seals, then we ought to regard Baptism as much greater and more precious because God has commanded it and, what is more, it is performed in his name. So the words read, "Go, baptize," not in your name but "in God's name."

To be baptized in God's name is to be baptized not by men   10 but by God himself. Although it is performed by men's hands, it is nevertheless truly God's own act. From this fact everyone can easily conclude that it is of much greater value than the work of any man or saint. For what work can man do that is greater than God's work?

Here the devil sets to work to blind us with false appearances   11 and lead us away from God's work to our own. It makes a much

---

[6] This was an argument used by some left-wing radicals in the sixteenth century.

more splendid appearance when a Carthusian[7] does many great and difficult works, and we all attach greater importance to our own achievements and merits. But the Scriptures teach that if we piled |2 together all the works of all the monks, no matter how precious and dazzling they might appear, they would not be as noble and good as if God were to pick up a straw. Why? Because the person performing the act is nobler and better. Here we must evaluate not the person according to the works, but the works according to the person, from whom they must derive their worth. But mad reason rushes forth[8] |3 and, because Baptism is not dazzling like the works which we do, regards it as worthless.

Now you can understand how to answer properly the question, |4 What is Baptism? It is not simply common water, but water comprehended in God's Word and commandment and sanctified by them. It is nothing else than a divine water, not that the water in itself is nobler than other water but that God's Word and commandment are added to it.

Therefore it is sheer wickedness and devilish blasphemy when |5 our new spirits, in order to slander Baptism, ignore God's Word and ordinance, consider nothing but the water drawn from the well, and then babble, "How can a handful of water help the soul?" Of |6 course, my friend! Who does not know that water is water, if such a separation is proper? But how dare you tamper thus with God's ordinance and tear from it the precious jeweled clasp with which God has fastened and enclosed it and from which he does not wish his ordinance to be separated? For the nucleus in the water is God's Word or commandment and God's name, and this is a treasure greater and nobler than heaven and earth.

Note the distinction, then: Baptism is a very different thing |7 from all other water, not by virtue of the natural substance but because here something nobler is added. God himself stakes his honor, his power, and his might on it. Therefore it is not simply a natural water, but a divine, heavenly, holy, and blessed water—praise it in any other terms you can—all by virtue of the Word, which is a heavenly, holy Word which no one can sufficiently extol, for it contains and conveys all the fullness of God. From the Word it derives its nature as a |8 sacrament, as St. Augustine taught, *"Accedat verbum ad elementum et fit sacramentum."* [9] This means that when the Word is added to the element or the natural substance, it becomes a sacrament, that is, a holy, divine thing and sign.

Therefore, we constantly teach that the sacraments and all the |9

---

[7] See above, Ten Commandments, 74 and footnote.

[8] Later version: But mad reason will not listen to this.

[9] *Tractate 80,* on John 3.

external things ordained and instituted by God should be regarded not according to the gross, external mask (as we see the shell of a nut) but as that in which God's Word is enclosed. In the same way   20 we speak about the parental estate and civil authority. If we regard these persons with reference to their noses, eyes, skin and hair, flesh and bones, they look no different from Turks and heathen. Someone might come and say, "Why should I think more of this person than of others?" But because the commandment is added, "You shall honor father and mother," I see another man, adorned and clothed with the majesty and glory of God. The commandment, I say, is the golden chain about his neck, yes, the crown on his head, which shows me how and why I should honor this particular flesh and blood.

In the same manner, and even much more, you should honor   21 and exalt Baptism on account of the Word, since God himself has honored it by words and deeds and has confirmed it by wonders from heaven. Do you think it was a jest that the heavens opened when Christ allowed himself to be baptized, that the Holy Spirit descended visibly,[1] and that the divine glory and majesty were manifested everywhere?

I therefore admonish you again that these two, the Word and   22 the water, must by no means be separated from each other. For where the Word is separated from the water, the water is no different from that which the maid cooks with and could indeed be called a bath-keeper's baptism.[2] But when the Word is present according to God's ordinance, Baptism is a sacrament, and it is called Christ's Baptism. This is the first point to be emphasized: the nature and dignity of this holy sacrament.

In the second place, since we now know what Baptism is and   23 how it is to be regarded, we must also learn for what purpose it was instituted, that is, what benefits, gifts, and effects it brings. Nor can we understand this better than from the words of Christ quoted above, "He who believes and is baptized shall be saved." [3] To put it   24 most simply, the power, effect, benefit, fruit, and purpose of Baptism is to save. No one is baptized in order to become a prince, but as the words say, to "be saved." To be saved, we know, is nothing   25 else than to be delivered from sin, death, and the devil and to enter into the kingdom of Christ and live with him forever.

Here you see again how precious and important a thing Baptism   26 should be regarded as being, for in it we obtain such an inexpressible treasure. This shows that it is not simple, ordinary water, for ordinary

---

[1] Matt. 3:16.
[2] Cf. Luther's "Sermon on Baptism" (1534): "a mere watery or earthly water, or (as the sectarians call it) a bath-water or dog's bath." *WA*, 37:642.
[3] Mark 16:16.

water could not have such an affect. But the Word has. It shows also (as we said above) that God's name is in it. And where God's 27 name is, there must also be life and salvation. Hence it is well described as a divine, blessed, fruitful, and gracious water, for through the Word Baptism receives the power to become the "washing of regeneration," as St. Paul calls it in Titus 3:5.

Our know-it-alls, the new spirits,[4] assert that faith alone saves 28 and that works and external things contribute nothing to this end. We answer: It is true, nothing that is in us does it but faith, as we shall hear later on. But these leaders of the blind are unwilling 29 to see that faith must have something to believe—something to which it may cling and upon which it may stand. Thus faith clings to the water and believes it to be Baptism in which there is sheer salvation and life, not through the water, as we have sufficiently stated, but through its incorporation with God's Word and ordinance and the joining of his name to it. When I believe this, what else is it but believing in God as the one who has implanted his Word in this external ordinance and offered it to us so that we may grasp the treasure it contains?

Now, these people are so foolish as to separate faith from 30 the object to which faith is attached and bound on the ground that the object is something external. Yes, it must be external so that it can be perceived and grasped by the senses and thus brought into the heart, just as the entire Gospel is an external, oral proclamation. In short, whatever God effects in us he does through such external ordinances. No matter where he speaks—indeed, no matter for what purpose or by what means he speaks—there faith must look and to it faith must hold. We have here the words, "He who believes and 31 is baptized will be saved." To what do they refer but to Baptism, that is, the water comprehended in God's ordinance? Hence it follows that whoever rejects Baptism rejects God's Word, faith, and Christ, who directs us and binds us to Baptism.

In the third place, having learned the great benefit and power 32 of Baptism, let us observe further who receives these gifts and benefits of Baptism. This again is most beautifully and clearly expressed 33 in these same words, "He who believes and is baptized will be saved," that is, faith alone makes the person worthy to receive the salutary, divine water profitably. Since these blessings are offered and promised in the words which accompany the water, they cannot be received unless we believe them whole-heartedly. Without faith Baptism 34 is of no use, although in itself it is an infinite, divine treasure. So this single expression, "He who believes," is so potent that it excludes and rejects all works that we may do with the intention of meriting salva-

[4] Zwinglians or Anabaptists.

tion through them. For it is certain that whatever is not faith con-
tributes nothing toward salvation, and receives nothing.

However, it is often objected, "If Baptism is itself a work, and   35
you say that works are of no use for salvation, what becomes of
faith?" To this you may answer: Yes, it is true that our works are
of no use for salvation. Baptism, however, is not our work but God's
(for, as was said, you must distinguish Christ's Baptism quite clearly
from a bath-keeper's baptism). God's works, however, are salutary
and necessary for salvation, and they do not exclude but rather demand[5] faith, for without faith they could not be grasped. Just by   36
allowing the water to be poured over you, you do not receive Baptism
in such a manner that it does you any good. But it becomes beneficial
to you if you accept it as God's command and ordinance, so that,
baptized in the name of God, you may receive in the water the
promised salvation. This the hand cannot do, nor the body, but the
heart must believe it.

Thus you see plainly that Baptism is not a work which we do   37
but is a treasure which God gives us and faith grasps, just as the Lord
Christ upon the cross is not a work but a treasure comprehended and
offered to us in the Word and received by faith. Therefore they are
unfair when they cry out against us as though we preach against faith.
Actually, we insist on faith alone as so necessary that without it nothing
can be received or enjoyed.

Thus we have considered the three things that must be known   38
about this sacrament, especially that it is God's ordinance and is to
be held in all honor. This alone would be enough, even though
Baptism is an entirely external thing. Similarly the commandment,
"You shall honor your father and mother," refers only to human
flesh and blood, yet we look not at the flesh and blood but at God's
commandment in which it is comprehended and on account of which
this flesh is called father and mother. Just so, if we had nothing more
than these words, "Go and baptize," we would still have to accept and
observe Baptism as an ordinance of God. But here we have not   39
only God's commandment and injunction, but also his promise. Therefore, it is far more glorious than anything else God has commanded
and ordained; in short, it is so full of comfort and grace that heaven
and earth cannot comprehend it. It takes special understanding   40
to believe this, for it is not the treasure that is lacking; rather, what is
lacking is that it should be grasped and held firmly.

In Baptism, therefore, every Christian has enough to study and   41
to practice all his life. He always has enough to do to believe firmly
what Baptism promises and brings—victory over death and the devil,

---

[5] Luther's word *fodern* may mean both "demand" (*forden*) and "further"
(*fördern*). Obsopoeus' Latin translation of the Catechism understood the
word here as "demand."

forgiveness of sin, God's grace, the entire Christ, and the Holy Spirit with his gifts. In short, the blessings of Baptism are so boundless 42 that if timid nature considers them, it may well doubt whether they could all be true. Suppose there were a physician who had such 43 skill that people would not die, or even though they died[6] would afterward live forever. Just think how the world would snow and rain money upon him! Because of the pressing crowd of rich men no one else could get near him. Now, here in Baptism there is brought free to every man's door just such a priceless medicine which swallows up death[7] and saves the lives of all men.

To appreciate and use Baptism aright, we must draw strength 44 and comfort from it when our sins or conscience oppress us, and we must retort, "But I am baptized! And if I am baptized, I have the promise that I shall be saved and have eternal life, both in soul and body." This is the reason why these two things are done in 45 Baptism: the body has water poured over it, though it cannot receive anything but the water, and meanwhile the Word is spoken so that the soul may grasp it.

Since the water and the Word together constitute one Baptism, 46 body and soul shall be saved and live forever: the soul through the Word in which it believes, the body because it is united with the soul and apprehends Baptism in the only way it can. No greater jewel, therefore, can adorn our body and soul than Baptism, for through it we obtain perfect holiness and salvation, which no other kind of life and no work on earth can acquire.

Let this suffice concerning the nature, benefits, and use of Baptism as answering the present purpose.

[INFANT BAPTISM] [8]

Here we come to a question by which the devil confuses the 47 world through his sects, the question of infant Baptism. Do children also believe, and is it right to baptize them? To this we reply 48 briefly: Let the simple dismiss this question from their minds and refer it to the learned. But if you wish to answer, then say:

That the Baptism of infants is pleasing to Christ is sufficiently 49 proved from his own work. God has sanctified many who have been thus baptized and has given them the Holy Spirit. Even today there are not a few whose doctrine and life attest that they have the Holy Spirit. Similarly by God's grace we have been given the power to interpret the Scriptures and to know Christ, which is impossible without the Holy Spirit. Now, if God did not accept the Baptism of 50

---

[6] Later version adds: would be restored to life and.
[7] Isa. 25:8.
[8] Title added in the German Book of Concord.

infants, he would not have given any of them the Holy Spirit nor any part of him; in short, all this time down to the present day no man on earth could have been a Christian. Since God has confirmed Baptism through the gift of his Holy Spirit, as we have perceived in some of the fathers, such as St. Bernard, Gerson, John Hus, and others,[9] and since the holy Christian church will abide until the end of the world, our adversaries must acknowledge that infant Baptism is pleasing to God. For he can never be in conflict with himself, support lies and wickedness, or give his grace and Spirit for such ends. This 51 is the best and strongest proof for the simple and unlearned. For no one can take from us or overthrow this article, "I believe one holy Christian church, the communion of saints," etc.

Further, we are not primarily concerned whether the baptized 52 person believes or not, for in the latter case Baptism does not become invalid. Everything depends upon the Word and commandment 53 of God. This, perhaps, is a rather subtle point, but it is based upon what I have already said, that Baptism is simply water and God's Word in and with each other; that is, when the Word accompanies the water, Baptism is valid, even though faith be lacking. For my faith does not constitute Baptism but receives it. Baptism does not become invalid even if it is wrongly received or used, for it is bound not to our faith but to the Word.

Even though a Jew should today come deceitfully and with 54 an evil purpose, and we baptized him in all good faith, we should have to admit that his Baptism was valid. For there would be water together with God's Word, even though he failed to receive it properly. Similarly, those who partake unworthily of the Lord's Supper receive the true sacrament even though they do not believe.

So you see that the objection of the sectarians is absurd. As 55 we said, even if infants did not believe—which, however, is not the case, as we have proved—still their Baptism would be valid and no one should rebaptize them. Similarly, the Sacrament of the Altar is not vitiated if someone approaches it with an evil purpose, and he would not be permitted on account of that abuse to take it again the selfsame hour, as if he had not really received the sacrament the first time. That would be to blaspheme and desecrate the sacrament in the worst way. How dare we think that God's Word and ordinance should be wrong and invalid because we use it wrongly?

Therefore, I say, if you did not believe before, then believe 56 afterward and confess, "The Baptism indeed was right, but unfortunately I did not receive it rightly." I myself, and all who are baptized, must say before God: "I come here in my faith, and in the faith of others, nevertheless I cannot build on the fact that I believe and

[9] Later version adds: who were baptized in infancy.

many people are praying for me. On this I build, that it is thy Word and command." Just so, I go to the Sacrament of the Altar not on the strength of my own faith, but on the strength of Christ's Word. I may be strong or weak; I leave that in God's hands. This I know, however, that he has commanded me to go, eat, and drink, etc. and that he gives me his body and blood; he will not lie or deceive me.

We do the same in infant Baptism. We bring the child with 57 the purpose and hope that he may believe, and we pray God to grant him faith. But we do not baptize him on that account, but solely on the command of God. Why? Because we know that God does not lie. My neighbor and I—in short, all men—may err and deceive, but God's Word cannot err.

Therefore only presumptuous and stupid persons draw the 58 conclusion that where there is no true faith, there also can be no true Baptism. Likewise I might argue, "If I have no faith, then Christ is nothing." Or again, "If I am not obedient, then father, mother, and magistrates are nothing." Is it correct to conclude that when anybody does not do what he should, the thing that he misuses has no existence or no value? My friend, rather invert the argument and conclude, 59 Precisely because Baptism has been wrongly received, it has existence and value. The saying goes, *"Abusus non tollit, sed confirmat substantiam,"* that is, "Misuse does not destroy the substance, but confirms its existence." Gold remains no less gold if a harlot wears it in sin and shame.

Let the conclusion therefore be that Baptism always remains 60 valid and retains its integrity, even if only one person were baptized and he, moreover, did not have true faith. For God's ordinance and Word cannot be changed or altered by man. But these fanatics 61 are so blinded that they do not discern God's Word and commandment. They regard Baptism only as water in the brook or in the pot, and magistrates only as ordinary people. And because they see neither faith nor obedience, they conclude that these ordinances are in themselves invalid. Here lurks a sneaky, seditious devil who would 62 like to snatch the crown from the rulers and trample it under foot and would, in addition, pervert and nullify all God's work and ordinances. We must therefore be watchful and well armed and not 63 allow ourselves to be turned aside from the Word, regarding Baptism merely as an empty sign, as the fanatics dream.

Finally, we must know what Baptism signifies and why God 64 ordained just this sign and external observance for the sacrament by which we are first received into the Christian church. This act or 65 observance consists in being dipped into the water, which covers us completely, and being drawn out again. These two parts, being dipped under the water and emerging from it, indicate the power and effect

of Baptism, which is simply the slaying of the old Adam and the
resurrection of the new man, both of which actions must continue in
us our whole life long. Thus a Christian life is nothing else than a
daily Baptism, once begun and ever continued. For we must keep
at it incessantly, always purging out whatever pertains to the old
Adam, so that whatever belongs to the new man may come forth.
What is the old man? He is what is born in us from Adam, 66
irascible, spiteful, envious, unchaste, greedy, lazy, proud, yes, and
unbelieving; he is beset with all vices and by nature has nothing good
in him. Now, when we enter Christ's kingdom, this corruption 67
must daily decrease so that the longer we live the more gentle, patient,
and meek we become, and the more free from greed, hatred, envy,
and pride.

This is the right use of Baptism among Christians, signified by 68
baptizing with water. Where this amendment of life does not take
place but the old man is given free rein and continually grows stronger,
Baptism is not being used but resisted. Those who are outside of 69
Christ can only grow worse day by day. It is as the proverb says
very truly, "Evil unchecked becomes worse and worse." If a year 70
ago a man was proud and greedy, this year he is much more so. Vice
thus grows and increases in him from his youth up. A young child,
who has no particular vice, becomes vicious and unchaste as he grows.
When he reaches full manhood, the real vices become more and more
potent day by day.

The old man therefore follows unchecked the inclinations of 71
his nature if he is not restrained and suppressed by the power of
Baptism. On the other hand, when we become Christians, the old man
daily decreases until he is finally destroyed. This is what it means to
plunge into Baptism and daily come forth again. So the external 72
sign has been appointed not only on account of what it confers, but
also on account of what it signifies. Where faith is present with its 73
fruits, there Baptism is no empty symbol, but the effect accompanies
it; but where faith is lacking, it remains a mere unfruitful sign.

Here you see that Baptism, both by its power and by its 74
signification, comprehends also the third sacrament, formerly called
Penance,[1] which is really nothing else than Baptism. What is 75
repentance but an earnest attack on the old man and an entering upon
a new life? If you live in repentance, therefore, you are walking in
Baptism, which not only announces this new life but also produces,
begins, and promotes it. In Baptism we are given the grace, Spirit, 76

---

[1] *Penitentia* (*Busse*) in the Roman Catholic system meant both the
sacrament (Penance) and the act of satisfaction enjoined by the priest
(penance) and the inward attitude of repentance.

and power to suppress the old man so that the new may come forth
and grow strong.

Therefore Baptism remains forever. Even though we fall from   77
it and sin, nevertheless we always have access to it so that we may
again subdue the old man. But we need not again have the water   78
poured over us. Even if we were immersed in water a hundred times, it
would nevertheless be only one Baptism, and the effect and signification
of Baptism would continue and remain. Repentance, therefore, is   79
nothing else than a return and approach to Baptism, to resume and
practice what had earlier been begun but abandoned.

I say this to correct the opinion, which has long prevailed   80
among us, that our Baptism is something past which we can no longer
use after falling again into sin. We have such a notion because we
regard Baptism only in the light of a work performed once for all.
Indeed, St. Jerome is responsible for this view, for he wrote,   81
"Repentance is the second plank[2] on which we must swim ashore after
the ship founders" in which we embarked when we entered the
Christian church.[3] This interpretation deprives Baptism of its   82
value, making it of no further use to us. Therefore the statement is
incorrect.[4] The ship does not founder since, as we said, it is God's
ordinance and not a work of ours. But it does happen that we slip
and fall out of the ship. If anybody does fall out, he should immediately
head for the ship and cling to it until he can climb aboard again and
sail on in it as he had done before.

Thus we see what a great and excellent thing Baptism is, which   83
snatches us from the jaws of the devil and makes God our own,
overcomes and takes away sin and daily strengthens the new man,
always remains until we pass from this present misery to eternal glory.

Therefore let everybody regard his Baptism as the daily   84
garment which he is to wear all the time. Every day he should be
found in faith and amid its fruits, every day he should be suppressing
the old man and growing up in the new. If we wish to be   85
Christians, we must practice the work that makes us Christians.
But if anybody falls away from his Baptism let him return to it.   86
As Christ, the mercy-seat,[5] does not recede from us or forbid us to
return to him even though we sin, so all his treasures and gifts remain.
As we have once obtained forgiveness of sins in Baptism, so forgiveness
remains day by day as long as we live, that is, as long as we carry
the old Adam about our necks.

---

[2] Baptism was regarded as the first plank.

[3] Epistle 130 to Demetrias. Cf. also Epistle 122 to Rusticus, Epistle 147 to
Fallen Sabinianus, and Commentary on Isaiah, ch. 3, 8-9.

[4] Later version adds: or else was never rightly understood.

[5] Cf. Rom. 3:25; Heb. 4:16.

[FIFTH PART:] THE SACRAMENT OF THE ALTAR

As we treated Holy Baptism under three headings, so we must 1
deal with the second sacrament in the same way, stating what it is,
what its benefits are, and who is to receive it. All these are established
from the words by which Christ instituted it. So everyone who 2
wishes to be a Christian and go to the sacrament should be familiar
with them. For we do not intend to admit to the sacrament and
administer it to those who do not know what they seek or why they
come. The words are these:

"Our Lord Jesus Christ on the night when he was betrayed took 3
bread, gave thanks, broke it, and gave it to his disciples and said,
'Take, eat; this is my body, which is given for you. Do this in
remembrance of me.'"

"In the same way also he took the cup, after supper, gave thanks,
and gave it to them, saying, 'This cup is the new testament in my
blood, which is poured out for you for the forgiveness of sins. Do this,
as often as you drink it, in remembrance of me.'" [6]

We have no wish on this occasion to quarrel and dispute with 4
those who blaspheme and desecrate this sacrament; but as in the case
of Baptism, we shall first learn what is of greatest importance, namely,
God's Word and ordinance or command, which is the chief thing
to be considered. For the Lord's Supper was not invented or devised
by any man. It was instituted by Christ without man's counsel or
deliberation. Therefore, just as the Ten Commandments, the 5
Lord's Prayer, and the Creed retain their nature and value even if we
never keep, pray, or believe them, so also does this blessed sacrament
remain unimpaired and inviolate even if we use and handle it unworthily. Do you think God cares so much about our faith and 6
conduct that he would permit them to affect his ordinance? No, all
temporal things remain as God has created and ordered them, regardless
of how we treat them. This must always be emphasized, for thus 7
we can thoroughly refute all the babbling of the seditious spirits who
regard the sacraments, contrary to the Word of God, as human
performances.

Now, what is the Sacrament of the Altar? Answer: It is the 8
true body and blood of the Lord Christ in and under the bread and
wine which we Christians are commanded by Christ's word to eat and
drink. As we said of Baptism that it is not mere water, so we say 9
here that the sacrament is bread and wine, but not mere bread or wine
such as is served at the table. It is bread and wine comprehended in
God's Word and connected with it.

[6] I Cor. 11:23-25; Matt. 26:26-28; Mark 14:22-24; Luke 22:19f.

It is the Word, I maintain, which distinguishes it from mere   10
bread and wine and constitutes it a sacrament which is rightly called
Christ's body and blood. It is said, *"Accedat verbum ad elementum et
fit sacramentum,"* that is, "When the Word is joined to the external
element, it becomes a sacrament." [7] This saying of St. Augustine is so
accurate and well put that it is doubtful if he has said anything better.
The Word must make the element a sacrament; otherwise it remains a
mere element. Now, this is not the word and ordinance of a   11
prince or emperor, but of the divine Majesty at whose feet every knee
should bow and confess that it is as he says and should accept it with
all reverence, fear, and humility.

With this Word you can strengthen your conscience and declare: 12
"Let a hundred thousand devils, with all the fanatics, rush forward
and say, 'How can bread and wine be Christ's body and blood?' Still
I know that all the spirits and scholars put together have less wisdom
than the divine Majesty has in his little finger. Here we have   13
Christ's word, 'Take, eat; this is my body.' 'Drink of it, all of you,
this is the new covenant in my blood,' etc. Here we shall take our
stand and see who dares to instruct Christ and alter what he has
spoken. It is true, indeed, that if you take the Word away from   14
the elements or view them apart from the Word, you have nothing but
ordinary bread and wine. But if the words remain, as is right and
necessary, then in virtue of them they are truly the body and blood
of Christ. For as we have it from the lips of Christ, so it is; he cannot
lie or deceive."

Hence it is easy to answer all kinds of questions which now   15
trouble men — for example, whether even a wicked priest can
administer the sacrament, and like questions. Our conclusion is: 16
Even though a knave should receive or administer it, it is the true
sacrament (that is, Christ's body and blood) just as truly as when one
uses it most worthily. For it is not founded on the holiness of men
but on the Word of God. As no saint on earth, yes, no angel in
heaven can transform bread and wine into Christ's body and blood, so
likewise no one can change or alter the sacrament, even if it is misused.
For the Word by which it was constituted a sacrament is not   17
rendered false because of an individual's unworthiness or unbelief.
Christ does not say, "If you believe, or if you are worthy, you receive
my body and blood," but, "Take, eat and drink, this is my body and
blood." Likewise, he says, "Do this," namely, what I now do, what I
institute, what I give you and bid you take. This is as much as to   18
say, "No matter whether you are unworthy or worthy, you here have
Christ's body and blood by virtue of these words which are coupled
with the bread and wine." Mark this and remember it well. For   19

[7] Cf. above, IV, Baptism, 18.

upon these words rest our whole argument, protection, and defense against all errors and deceptions that have ever arisen or may yet arise.

We have briefly considered the first part, namely, the essence   20 of this sacrament. Now we come to its power and benefit, the purpose for which the sacrament was really instituted, for it is most necessary that we know what we should seek and obtain there. This is   21 plainly evident from the words just quoted, "This is my body and blood, given and poured out *for you* for the forgiveness of sins." In other words, we go to the sacrament because we receive there   22 a great treasure, through and in which we obtain the forgiveness of sins. Why? Because the words are there through which this is imparted! Christ bids me eat and drink in order that the sacrament may be mine and may be a source of blessing to me as a sure pledge and sign— indeed, as the very gift he has provided for me against my sins, death, and all evils.

Therefore, it is appropriately called the food of the soul since   23 it nourishes and strengthens the new man. While it is true that through Baptism we are first born anew, our human flesh and blood have not lost their old skin. There are so many hindrances and temptations of the devil and the world that we often grow weary and faint, at times even stumble. The Lord's Supper is given as a   24 daily food and sustenance so that our faith may refresh and strengthen itself and not weaken in the struggle but grow continually stronger. For the new life should be one that continually develops and   25 progresses. Meanwhile it must suffer much opposition. The devil   26 is a furious enemy; when he sees that we resist him and attack the old man, and when he cannot rout us by force, he sneaks and skulks about everywhere, trying all kinds of tricks, and does not stop until he has finally worn us out so that we either renounce our faith or yield hand and foot and become indifferent or impatient. For such   27 times, when our heart feels too sorely pressed, this comfort of the Lord's Supper is given to bring us new strength and refreshment.

Here again our clever spirits contort themselves with their   28 great learning and wisdom, bellowing and blustering, "How can bread and wine forgive sins or strengthen faith?" Yet they know that we do not claim this of bread and wine—since in itself bread is bread—but of that bread and wine which are Christ's body and blood and with which the words are coupled. These and no other, we say, are the treasure through which forgiveness is obtained. This treasure is conveyed   29 and communicated to us in no other way than through the words, "given and poured out for you." Here you have both truths, that it is Christ's body and blood and that these are yours as your treasure and gift. Christ's body can never be an unfruitful, vain thing, impotent   30 and useless. Yet, however great the treasure may be in itself, it must be comprehended in the Word and offered to us through the Word, otherwise we could never know of it or seek it.

Therefore it is absurd to say that Christ's body and blood are   31 not given and poured out for us in the Lord's Supper and hence that we cannot have forgiveness of sins in the sacrament. Although the work was accomplished and forgiveness of sins was acquired on the cross, yet it cannot come to us in any other way than through the Word. How should we know that this has been accomplished and offered to us if it were not proclaimed by preaching, by the oral Word? Whence do they know of forgiveness, and how can they grasp and appropriate it, except by steadfastly believing the Scriptures and the Gospel? Now, the whole Gospel and the article of the Creed, "I   32 believe in the holy Christian church, the forgiveness of sins," are embodied in this sacrament and offered to us through the Word. Why, then, should we allow this treasure to be torn out of the sacrament? Our opponents[8] must still confess that these are the very words which we hear everywhere in the Gospel. They can say that these words in the sacrament are of no value just as little as they dare say that the whole Gospel or Word of God apart from the sacrament is of no value.

So far we have treated the sacrament from the standpoint both   33 of its essence and of its effect and benefit. It remains for us to consider who it is that receives this power and benefit. Briefly, as we said above concerning Baptism and in many other places, the answer is: It is he who believes what the words say and what they give, for they are not spoken or preached to stone and wood but to those who hear them, those to whom Christ says, "Take and eat," etc. And   34 because he offers and promises forgiveness of sins, it cannot be received except by faith. This faith he himself demands in the Word when he says, "Given *for you*" and "poured out *for you*," as if he said, "This is why I give it and bid you eat and drink, that you may take it as your own and enjoy it." Whoever lets these words be addressed   35 to him and believes that they are true has what the words declare. But he who does not believe has nothing, for he lets this gracious blessing be offered to him in vain and refuses to enjoy it. The treasure is opened and placed at everyone's door, yes, upon everyone's table, but it is also your responsibility to take it and confidently believe that it is just as the words tell you.

This, now, is the preparation required of a Christian for   36 receiving this sacrament worthily. Since this treasure is fully offered in the words, it can be grasped and appropriated only by the heart. Such a gift and eternal treasure cannot be seized with the hand. Fasting and prayer and the like may have their place as an   37

---

[8] Zwinglians and Anabaptists.

external preparation and children's exercise so that one's body may behave properly and reverently toward the body and blood of Christ. But what is given in and with the sacrament cannot be grasped and appropriated by the body. This is done by the faith of the heart which discerns and desires this treasure.

Enough has been said now for all ordinary instruction on the   38 essentials of this sacrament. What may further be said about it belongs to another occasion.

In conclusion, now that we have the right interpretation and   39 doctrine of the sacrament, there is great need also of an admonition and entreaty that so great a treasure, which is daily administered and distributed among Christians, may not be heedlessly passed by. What I mean is that those who claim to be Christians should prepare themselves to receive this blessed sacrament frequently. For we see   40 that men are becoming listless and lazy about its observance. A lot of people who hear the Gospel, now that the pope's nonsense has been abolished and we are freed from his oppression and authority, let a year, or two, three, or more years go by without receiving the sacrament, as if they were such strong Christians that they have no need of it. Some let themselves be kept and deterred from it   41 because we have taught that no one should go unless he feels a hunger and thirst impelling him to it. Some pretend that it is a matter of liberty, not of necessity, and that it is enough if they simply believe. Thus the majority go so far that they become quite barbarous, and ultimately despise both the sacrament and the Word of God.

Now it is true, we repeat, that no one should under any   42 circumstances be coerced or compelled, lest we institute a new slaughter of souls. Nevertheless, let it be understood that people who abstain and absent themselves from the sacrament over a long period of time are not to be considered Christians. Christ did not institute it to be treated merely as a spectacle, but commanded his Christians to eat and drink and thereby remember him.

Indeed, true Christians who cherish and honor the sacrament   43 will of their own accord urge and impel themselves to come. However, in order that the common people and the weak, who also would like to be Christians, may be induced to see the reason and the need for receiving the sacrament, we shall devote a little attention to this point. As in other matters pertaining to faith, love, and patience it is   44 not enough simply to teach and instruct, but there must also be daily exhortation, so on this subject we must be persistent in preaching, lest people become indifferent and bored. For we know from experience that the devil always sets himself against this and every other Christian activity, hounding and driving people from it as much as he can.

In the first place, we have a clear text in the words of Christ,   45 "*Do this* in remembrance of me." These are words of precept and

command, enjoining all who would be Christians to partake of the
sacrament. They are words addressed to disciples of Christ; hence
whoever would be one of them, let him faithfully hold to this sacrament, not from compulsion, coerced by men, but to obey and please
the Lord Christ. However, you may say, "But the words are   46
added, 'as often as you do it'; so he compels no one, but leaves it to
our free choice." I answer: That is true, but it does not say that   47
we should never partake. Indeed, the very words, "as often as you do
it," imply that we should do it often. And they are added because
Christ wishes the sacrament to be free, not bound to a special time
like the Passover, which the Jews were obliged to eat only once a year,
precisely on the evening of the fourteenth day of the first full moon,[9]
without variation of a single day. Christ means to say: "I institute a
Passover or Supper for you, which you shall enjoy not just on this one
evening of the year, but frequently, whenever and wherever you will,
according to everyone's opportunity and need, being bound to no
special place or time" (although the pope afterward perverted it   48
and turned it back into a Jewish feast).[1]

Thus you see that we are not granted liberty to despise the   49
sacrament. When a person, with nothing to hinder him, lets a long
period of time elapse without ever desiring the sacrament, I call that
despising it. If you want such liberty, you may just as well take the
further liberty not to be a Christian; then you need not believe or pray,
for the one is just as much Christ's commandment as the other. But
if you wish to be a Christian, you must from time to time satisfy and
obey this commandment. For this commandment should ever   50
move you to examine your inner life and reflect: "See what sort of
Christian I am! If I were one, I would surely have at least a little
longing to do what my Lord has commanded me to do."

Indeed, since we show such an aversion toward the sacrament,   51
men can easily sense what sort of Christians we were under the papacy
when we attended the sacrament merely from compulsion and fear of
men's commandments, without joy and love and even without regard
for Christ's commandment. But we neither force nor compel   52
anyone, nor need anyone partake of the sacrament to serve or please
us. What should move and impel you is the fact that Christ desires it,
and it pleases him. You should not let yourself be forced by men
either to faith or to any good work. All we are doing is to urge you
to do what you ought to do, not for our sake but for your own. He
invites and incites you; if you despise this, you must answer for it
yourself.

[9] Lev. 23:5.
[1] Cf. Fourth Lateran Council (1215): "receiving reverently the sacrament
of the Eucharist at least in Paschal time. . . ." Henry Denzinger, *The Sources
of Catholic Dogma,* tr. R. J. Deferrari (1957), p. 173.

This is the first point, especially for the benefit of the cold and 53 indifferent, that they may come to their senses and wake up. It is certainly true, as I have found in my own experience, and as everyone will find in his own case, that if a person stays away from the sacrament, day by day he will become more and more callous and cold, and eventually spurn it altogether. To avoid this, we must 54 examine our heart and conscience and act like a person who really desires to be right with God. The more we do this, the more will our heart be warmed and kindled, and it will not grow entirely cold.

But suppose you say, "What if I feel that I am unfit?" Answer: 55 This also is my temptation, especially inherited from the old order under the pope when we tortured ourselves to become so perfectly pure that God might not find the least blemish in us. Because of this we became so timid that everyone was thrown into consternation, saying, "Alas, I am not worthy!" Then nature and reason begin 56 to contrast our unworthiness with this great and precious blessing, and it appears like a dark lantern in contrast to the bright sun, or as dung in contrast to jewels. Because nature and reason see this, such people refuse to go to the sacrament and wait until they become prepared, until one week passes into another and one half year into yet another. If you choose to fix your eye on how good and pure 57 you are, to work toward the time when nothing will prick your conscience, you will never go.

For this reason we must make a distinction among men. Those 58 who are shameless and unruly must be told to stay away, for they are not fit to receive the forgiveness of sins since they do not desire it and do not want to be good. The others, who are not so callous 59 and dissolute but would like to be good, should not absent themselves, even though in other respects they are weak and frail. As St. Hilary has said, "Unless a man has committed such a sin that he has forfeited the name of Christian and has to be expelled from the congregation, he should not exclude himself from the sacrament," lest he deprive himself of life.[2] No one will make such progress 60 that he does not retain many common infirmities in his flesh and blood.

People with such misgivings must learn that it is the highest 61 wisdom to realize that this sacrament does not depend upon our worthiness. We are not baptized because we are worthy and holy, nor do we come to confession pure and without sin; on the contrary, we come as poor, miserable men, precisely because we are unworthy. The only exception is the person who desires no grace and absolution and has no intention to amend his life.

[2] Gratian, *Decretum*, Pt. III, D. 2, c. 15, quotes Hilary: "If a man's sins are not so great as to require excommunication, he must not exclude himself from the medicine of the Lord's body." The passage, however, is to be found in Augustine, Epistle 54, c. 3.

He who earnestly desires grace and consolation should compel   62
himself to go and allow no one to deter him, saying, "I would really
like to be worthy, but I come not on account of any worthiness of
mine, but on account of thy Word, because Thou hast commanded it
and I want to be thy disciple, no matter how insignificant my
worthiness." This is difficult, for we always have this obstacle and   63
hindrance to contend with, that we concentrate more upon ourselves
than upon the words that proceed from Christ's lips. Nature would like
to act in such a way that it may rest and rely firmly upon itself;
otherwise it refuses to take a step. Let this suffice for the first point.

In the second place, a promise is attached to the commandment,   64
as we heard above, which should most powerfully draw and impel us.
Here stand the gracious and lovely words, "This is my body, given
for you," "This is my blood, poured out *for you* for the forgiveness
of sins." These words, I have said, are not preached to wood or   65
stone but to you and me; otherwise Christ might just as well have
kept quiet and not instituted a sacrament. Ponder, then, and include
yourself personally in the "you" so that he may not speak to you in
vain.

In this sacrament he offers us all the treasure he brought from   66
heaven for us, to which he most graciously invites us in other places,
as when he says in Matt. 11:28, "Come to me, all who labor and are
heavy-laden, and I will refresh you." Surely it is a sin and a shame   67
that, when he tenderly and faithfully summons and exhorts us to our
highest and greatest good, we act so distantly toward it, neglecting it
so long that we grow quite cold and callous and lose all desire and
love for it. We must never regard the sacrament as a harmful   68
thing from which we should flee, but as a pure, wholesome, soothing
medicine which aids and quickens us in both soul and body. For
where the soul is healed, the body has benefited also. Why, then,
do we act as if the sacrament were a poison which would kill us if
we ate of it?

Of course, it is true that those who despise the sacrament and   69
lead unchristian lives receive it to their harm and damnation. To
such people nothing can be good or wholesome, just as when a sick
person willfully eats and drinks what is forbidden him by the
physician. But those who feel their weakness, who are anxious to   70
be rid of it and desire help, should regard and use the sacrament as a
precious antidote against the poison in their systems. For here in the
sacrament you receive from Christ's lips the forgiveness of sins, which
contains and conveys God's grace and Spirit with all his gifts,
protection, defense, and power against death and the devil and all evils.

Thus you have on God's part both the commandment and the   71
promise of the Lord Christ. Meanwhile, on your part, you ought to be
impelled by your own need, which hangs around your neck and which

is the very reason for this command and invitation and promise. Christ himself says, "Those who are well have no need of a physician, but those who are sick," [3] that is, those who labor and are heavy-laden with sin, fear of death, and the assaults of the flesh and the devil. If you are heavy-laden and feel your weakness, go joyfully to the 72 sacrament and receive refreshment, comfort, and strength. If you 73 wait until you are rid of your burden in order to come to the sacrament purely and worthily, you must stay away from it forever. In such a case Christ pronounces the judgment, "If you are pure 74 and upright, you have no need of me and I have no need of you." Therefore they alone are unworthy who neither feel their infirmities nor admit to being sinners.

Suppose you say, "What shall I do if I cannot feel this need or 75 experience hunger and thirst for the sacrament?" Answer: For persons in such a state of mind that they cannot feel it, I know no better advice than to suggest that they put their hands to their bosom and ask whether they are made of flesh and blood. If you find that you are, then for your own good turn to St. Paul's Epistle to the Galatians and hear what are the fruits of the flesh: "The works of the flesh are plain: adultery, immorality, impurity, licentiousness, idolatry, sorcery, enmity, strife, jealousy, anger, selfishness, dissension, party spirit, envy, murder, drunkenness, carousing, and the like." [4]

If you cannot feel the need, therefore, at least believe the 76 Scriptures. They will not lie to you, and they know your flesh better than you yourself do. Yes, and St. Paul concludes in Rom. 7:18, "For I know that nothing good dwells within me, that is, in my flesh." If St. Paul can speak thus of his flesh, let us not pretend to be better or more holy. But the fact that we are insensitive to our sin is all 77 the worse, for it is a sign that ours is a leprous flesh which feels nothing though the disease rages and rankles. As we have said, 78 even if you are so utterly dead in sin, at least believe the Scriptures, which pronounce this judgment upon you. In short, the less you feel your sins and infirmities, the more reason you have to go to the sacrament and seek a remedy.

Again, look about you and see whether you are also in the 79 world. If you do not know, ask your neighbors about it. If you are in the world, do not think that there will be any lack of sins and needs. Just begin to act as if you want to become good and cling to the Gospel, and see whether you will not acquire enemies who harm, wrong, and injure you and give you occasion for sin and wrong-doing. If you have not experienced this, then take it from the Scriptures, which everywhere give this testimony about the world.

[3] Matt. 9:12.
[4] Gal. 5:19, 20.

Besides the flesh and the world, you will surely have the devil   80
about you. You will not entirely trample him under foot because
our Lord Christ himself could not entirely avoid him. Now, what   81
is the devil? Nothing else than what the Scriptures call him, a liar
and a murderer.[5] A liar who seduces the heart from God's Word and
blinds it, making you unable to feel your needs or come to Christ. A
murderer who begrudges you every hour of your life. If you could   82
see how many daggers, spears, and arrows are at every moment aimed
at you, you would be glad to come to the sacrament as often as
possible. The only reason we go about so securely and heedlessly is
that we neither acknowledge nor believe that we are in the flesh, in
this wicked world, or under the kingdom of the devil.

Try this, therefore, and practice it well. Just examine yourself,   83
look around a little, cling to the Scriptures. If even then you feel
nothing, you have all the more need to lament both to God and to
your brother. Take others' advice and seek their prayers, and never
give up until the stone is removed from your heart. Then your   84
need will become apparent, and you will perceive that you have sunk
twice as low as any other poor sinner and are much in need of the
sacrament to combat your misery. This misery, unfortunately, you
do not see, though God grants his grace that you may become more
sensitive to it and more hungry for the sacrament. This happens
especially because the devil so constantly besieges you and lies in wait
to trap and destroy you, soul and body, so that you cannot be safe
from him one hour. How quickly can he bring you into misery and
distress when you least expect it!

Let this serve as an exhortation, then, not only for us who are   85
grown and advanced in years, but also for the young people who
ought to be brought up in Christian doctrine and a right understanding
of it. With such training we may more easily instill the Ten
Commandments, the Creed, and the Lord's Prayer into the young
so that they will receive them with joy and earnestness, practice them
from their youth, and become accustomed to them. For it is   86
clearly useless to try to change old people. We cannot perpetuate
these and other teachings unless we train the people who come after
us and succeed us in our office and work, so that they in turn may
bring up their children successfully. Thus the Word of God and the
Christian church will be preserved. Therefore let every head of a   87
household remember that it is his duty, by God's injunction and
command, to teach or have taught to his children the things they
ought to know. Since they are baptized and received into the Christian
church, they should also enjoy this fellowship of the sacrament so that

[5] John 8:44.

they may serve us and be useful. For they must all help us to believe, to love, to pray, and to fight the devil.

Here follows an exhortation to confession.[6]

A Brief Exhortation to Confession

Concerning confession, we have always taught that it should be 1 voluntary and purged of the pope's tyranny. We have been set free from his coercion and from the intolerable burden he imposed upon the Christian church. Up to now, as we all know from experience, there has been no law quite so oppressive as that which forced everyone to make confession on pain of the gravest mortal sin. Moreover, it so greatly burdened and tortured consciences with the 2 enumeration of all kinds of sin that no one was able to confess purely enough. Worst of all, no one taught or understood what confession 3 is and how useful and comforting it is. Instead, it was made sheer anguish and a hellish torture since people had to make confession even though nothing was more hateful to them. These three things 4 have now been removed and made voluntary so that we may confess without coercion or fear, and we are released from the torture of enumerating all sins in detail. Moreover, we have the advantage of knowing how to use confession beneficially for the comforting and strengthening of our conscience.

Everyone knows this now. Unfortunately, men have learned it 5 only too well; they do whatever they please and take advantage of their freedom, acting as if they will never need or desire to go to confession any more. We quickly understand whatever benefits us, and we grasp with uncommon ease whatever in the Gospel is mild and gentle. But such pigs, as I have said, are unworthy to appear in the presence of the Gospel or to have any part of it. They ought to remain under the pope and submit to being driven and tormented to confess, fast, etc., more than ever before. For he who will not believe the Gospel, live according to it, and do what a Christian ought to do, should enjoy none of its benefits. What would happen if 6 you wished to enjoy the Gospel's benefits but did nothing about it and paid nothing for it? For such people we shall provide no preaching, nor will they have our permission to share and enjoy any part of our liberty, but we shall let the pope or his like bring them back into subjection and coerce them like the tyrant he is. The rabble who will not obey the Gospel deserve just such a jailer as God's devil and hangman. To others who hear it gladly, however, we must always 7 preach, exhorting, encouraging, and persuading them not to lose this

---

[6] The section on confession was added first in the 1529 revised edition of the Catechism. It was omitted in the Jena edition of Luther's Works and in the German Book of Concord, hence also in several later editions of the Catechism.

precious and comforting treasure which the Gospel offers. Therefore we must say something about confession to instruct and admonish the simple folk.

To begin with, I have said that in addition to the confession 8 which we are discussing here there are two other kinds, which have an even greater right to be called the Christians' common confession. I refer to the practice of confessing to God alone or to our neighbor alone, begging for forgiveness. These two kinds are expressed in the Lord's Prayer when we say, "Forgive us our debts, as we forgive our debtors," etc. Indeed, the whole Lord's Prayer is nothing else than 9 such a confession. For what is our prayer but a confession that we neither have nor do what we ought and a plea for grace and a happy conscience? This kind of confession should and must take place incessantly as long as we live. For this is the essence of a genuinely Christian life, to acknowledge that we are sinners and to pray for grace.

Similarly the second confession, which each Christian makes 10 toward his neighbor, is included in the Lord's Prayer. We are to confess our guilt before one another and forgive one another before we come into God's presence to beg for forgiveness. Now, all of us are debtors one to another, therefore we should and we may confess publicly in everyone's presence, no one being afraid of anyone else. For it is true, as the proverb says, "If one man is upright, so are 11 they all"; no one does to God or his neighbor what he ought. However, besides our universal guilt there is also a particular one, when a person has provoked another to anger and needs to beg his pardon. Thus we have in the Lord's Prayer a twofold absolution: 12 our debts both to God and to our neighbor are forgiven when we forgive our neighbor and become reconciled with him.

Besides this public, daily, and necessary confession, there is 13 also the secret confession which takes place privately before a single brother. When some problem or quarrel sets us at one another's throats and we cannot settle it, and yet we do not find ourselves sufficiently strong in faith, we may at any time and as often as we wish lay our complaint before a brother, seeking his advice, comfort, and strength. This type of confession is not included in the command- 14 ment like the other two but is left to everyone to use whenever he needs it. Thus by divine ordinance Christ himself has entrusted absolution to his Christian church and commanded us to absolve one another from sins.[7] So if there is a heart that feels its sin and desires consolation, it has here a sure refuge when it hears in God's Word that through a man God looses and absolves him from his sins.

Note, then, as I have often said, that confession consists of 15 two parts. The first is my work and act, when I lament my sin and

[7] Matt. 18:15-19.

desire comfort and restoration for my soul. The second is a work which God does, when he absolves me of my sins through a word placed in the mouth of a man. This is the surpassingly grand and noble thing that makes confession so wonderful and comforting. In the past we placed all the emphasis on our work alone, and we   16 were only concerned whether we had confessed purely enough. We neither noticed nor preached the very necessary second part; it was just as if our confession were simply a good work with which we could satisfy God. Where the confession was not made perfectly and in complete detail, we were told that the absolution was not valid and the sin was not forgiven. Thereby the people were driven to the   17 point that everyone inevitably despaired of confessing so purely (which was impossible), and nobody could feel his conscience at peace or have confidence in his absolution. Thus the precious confession was not only made useless to us but it also became burdensome and bitter, to the manifest harm and destruction of souls.

We should therefore take care to keep the two parts clearly   18 separate. We should set little value on our work but exalt and magnify God's Word. We should not act as if we wanted to perform a magnificent work to present to him, but simply to accept and receive something from him. You dare not come and say how good or how wicked you are. If you are a Christian, I know this well enough   19 anyway; if you are not, I know it still better. But what you must do is to lament your need and allow yourself to be helped so that you may attain a happy heart and conscience.

Further, no one dare oppress you with requirements. Rather,   20 whoever is a Christian, or would like to be one, has here the faithful advice to go and obtain this precious treasure. If you are no Christian, and desire no such comfort, we shall leave you to another's power. Hereby we abolish the pope's tyranny, commandments, and   21 coercion since we have no need of them. For our teaching, as I have said, is this: If anybody does not go to confession willingly and for the sake of absolution, let him just forget about it. Yes, and if anybody goes about relying on the purity of his confession, let him just stay away from it. We urge you, however, to confess and express your   22 needs, not for the purpose of performing a work but to hear what God wishes to say to you. The Word or absolution, I say, is what you should concentrate on, magnifying and cherishing it as a great and wonderful treasure to be accepted with all praise and gratitude.

If all this were clearly explained, and meanwhile if the needs   23 which ought to move and induce us to confession were clearly indicated, there would be no need of coercion and force. A man's own conscience would impel him and make him so anxious that he would rejoice and act like a poor, miserable beggar who hears that a rich gift, of money or clothes, is to be given out at a certain place; he would need no bailiff to drive and beat him but would run there as fast as he could so as not to miss the gift. Suppose, now, that the invitation were 24 changed into a command that all beggars should run to the place, no reason being given and no mention of what they were to look for or receive. How else would the beggar go but with repugnance, not expecting to receive anything but just letting everyone see how poor and miserable he is? Not much joy or comfort would come from this, but only a greater hostility to the command.

In the same way the pope's preachers have in the past kept 25 silence about this wonderful, rich alms and this indescribable treasure; they have simply driven men together in hordes just to show what impure and filthy people they were. Who could thus go to confession willingly? We, on the contrary, do not say that men should look 26 to see how full of filthiness you are, making of you a mirror for contemplating themselves. Rather we advise: If you are poor and miserable, then go and make use of the healing medicine. He who 27 feels his misery and need will develop such a desire for confession that he will run toward it with joy. But those who ignore it and do not come of their own accord, we let go their way. However, they ought to know that we do not regard them as Christians.

Thus we teach what a wonderful, precious, and comforting 28 thing confession is, and we urge that such a precious blessing should not be despised, especially when we consider our great need. If you are a Christian, you need neither my compulsion nor the pope's command at any point, but you will compel yourself and beg me for the privilege of sharing in it. However, if you despise it and 29 proudly stay away from confession, then we must come to the conclusion that you are no Christian and that you ought not receive the sacrament. For you despise what no Christian ought to despise, and you show thereby that you can have no forgiveness of sin. And this is a sure sign that you also despise the Gospel.

In short, we approve of no coercion. However, if anyone 30 refuses to hear and heed the warning of our preaching, we shall have nothing to do with him, nor may he have any share in the Gospel. If you are a Christian, you should be glad to run more than a hundred miles for confession, not under compulsion but rather coming and compelling us to offer it. For here the compulsion must be 31 inverted; we must come under the command and you must come into freedom. We compel no man, but allow ourselves to be compelled, just as we are compelled to preach and administer the sacrament.

Therefore, when I urge you to go to confession, I am simply 32 urging you to be a Christian. If I bring you to this point, I have also brought you to confession. Those who really want to be good Christians, free from their sins, and happy in their conscience, already have

the true hunger and thirst. They snatch at the bread just like a
hunted hart, burning with heat and thirst, as Ps. 42:2 says, "As a   33
hart longs for flowing streams, so longs my soul for thee, O God."
That is, as a hart trembles with eagerness for a fresh spring, so I yearn
and tremble for God's Word, absolution, the sacrament, etc. In 34
this way, you see, confession would be rightly taught, and such a desire
and love for it would be aroused that people would come running after
us to get it, more than we would like. We shall let the papists torment
and torture themselves and other people who ignore such a treasure and
bar themselves from it. As for ourselves, however, let us lift our   35
hands in praise and thanks to God that we have attained to this blessed
knowledge of confession.